Sensory Awareness and Social Work

Sensory Awareness and Social Work

MICHELLE EVANS

AND

ANDREW WHITTAKER

Series Editors: Jonathan Parker and Greta Bradley

First published in 2010 by Learning Matters Ltd

British Library Cataloguing in Publication Data

A CIP record for this book is available from the British Library

ISBN 978 1 84445 291 0

This book is also available in the following ebook formats:
Adobe ebook ISBN 978 1 84445 665 9
EPUB ebook ISBN 978 1 84445 664 2
Kindle ISBN 978 1 84445 973 5

Text and cover design by Code 5 Design Associates
Project Management by Deer Park Productions, Tavistock, Devon
Typeset by Pantek Arts Ltd, Maidstone
Printed and bound in Great Britain by Bell & Bain Ltd, Glasgow

Learning Matters Ltd
33 Southernhay East
Exeter EX1 1NX
Tel: 01392 215560
E-mail: info@learningmatters.co.uk
www.learningmatters.co.uk

Contents

Acknowledgements

Michelle Evans would like to say a special thank you to all the specialist sensory organisations that provide never ending support to professionals and people with sensory needs and especially to those who feature in this book. Thanks also has to go to individuals whom she feels have been a sensory inspiration namely Tricia Pereira, Beryl Palmer, Julie Brown, Brian Eales, Michael Sadowski, June Smith and Alan Murray.

The Learning Matters staff, in particular Luke Block, Kate Lodge, Di Page and Jonathan Parker who have been an asset in the production of this book.

Certain people have been an inspiration during her social work career namely Tricia Pereira, Feargal Brady, Winsome Collins, Jean Kelly, Maureen Harding, Annie Knight, Xanthe Hyland, Nigel Cox, Gretchen Gamstradt, Sheila Will, Jane Bayliss, Annie Wilson and Graham Smith. They have shown her what good practice and integrity can achieve.

She would like to thank the London South Bank University, University of Kent and Canterbury Christ Church University teams who have had a huge impact on her career development, and really do promote equality and diversity and encourage people to be what they want to be.

She would also like to thank Bob Cecil and Toyin Okitikpi who were early academic inspirations. Iain Campbell King, Louise O'Connor, Alison Higgs, Tirion Harvard, Annabel Goodyer, David Shemmings, Vince Miller and Mark Oldfield continue to inspire.

Her love also goes to her Mum, Dad, brother, Joe, Sophie, Grant, Amelia, Francesca, Felicity, the Moore and Evans families and my friends (they know who they are). However, her deepest love and special appreciation goes to Alan and Jack for their never ending loving support and encouragement during the writing of this book.

Andrew Whittaker would like to give a particular thanks to Jill Yates and to his supportive colleagues at London South Bank University, namely Iain Campbell-King, Annabel Goodyer, Andrea Colquhoun, Martyn Higgins, Carl Chandra, Mary Saunders, Keith Popple, John Macdonough, Tom Wilks, Baljit Soroya, Tirion Havard, Claire Felix , Ruth Watson, Liz Green, Livia Horsham, Jo Rawles, Jonathan Davies, Wijaya Mallikaaratchi and Rose Stark. He would also like to thank his new colleagues at the Tavistock Clinic, Stephen Briggs and David Lawlor. He has appreciated the support of staff at Learning Matters, particularly Luke Block, Kate Lodge, Di Page and Jonathan Parker who have always been helpful and encouraging.

He would like to thank his father and mother for their love and for always being there for him. He would like to express thanks to his sister, Sally and her family, Joe, Ben and Lauren-Kate Mahmood for their love and warmth and for always cheering him on from the sidelines. He would like to thank his stepdaughters, Samantha and Rebecca, as well as Jonathan and Lily who all continue to look on with patient bemusement at his trips to the British Library. But most of all, he would like to thank Christina for her deep and unwavering love and for the happiness that comes with a shared life together.

Introduction

This book is written for student social workers who are beginning to develop their skills and understanding of the requirements for practice. It is aimed at undergraduate and postgraduate students who would like to raise their awareness in sensory issues. This book will also be useful for subsequent practice when working with an adult or child who has a sensory need. The book will also appeal to people considering a career in social work or social care but not yet studying for a social work degree. It will assist students undertaking a range of social and health care courses in further education. Nurses, occupational therapists and other health and social care professionals will be able to gain an insight into the new requirements demanded of social workers. Experienced and qualified social workers, especially those contributing to practice learning, will also be able to use this book for consultation, teaching, revision and to gain an insight into the expectations raised by the qualifying degree in social work.

Requirements for social work education

Social work education has undergone a major transformation to ensure that qualified social workers are educated to honours degree level and develop knowledge, skills and values which are common and shared. A vision for social work operating in complex human situations has been adopted. This is reflected in the following definition from the International Association of Schools of Social Work and International Federation of Social Workers (2001):

> The social work profession promotes social change, problem solving in human relationships and the empowerment and liberation of people to enhance well-being.

> Utilising theories of human behaviour and social systems, social work intervenes at the points where people interact with their environments. Principles of human rights and social justice are fundamental to social work.

While there is a great deal packed into this short and pithy definition, it encapsulates the notion that social work concerns individual people and wider society. Social workers practise with people who are vulnerable, who are struggling in some way to participate fully in society. Social workers walk that tightrope between the marginalised individual and the social and political environment that may have contributed to their marginalisation.

Social workers need to be highly skilled and knowledgeable to work effectively in this context. Therefore the government, together with organisations such as the Association of Directors of Adult Social Services (www.adass.org.uk) the Children's Workforce Development Council (www.cwdcouncil.org.uk), the Social Work Taskforce (www.dcsf. gov.uk/swtf), the British Association of Social Workers (www.basw.co.uk) and the General Social Care Council (www.gscc.org.uk) are keen for social work education and practice to improve. In order to improve the quality of both these aspects of professional social work, it is crucial that you, as a student social worker, develop a rigorous grounding in and understanding of theories and models for social work. Such knowledge helps social workers to know what to do, when to do it and how to do it, while recognising that social work is a complex activity with no absolute 'rights' and 'wrongs' of practice for each situation. We also concur with the Minister in championing the practical focus of social work, of being able to apply our knowledge to help others.

> *Social work is a very practical job. It is about protecting people and changing their lives, not about being able to give a fluent and theoretical explanation of why they got into difficulties in the first place. New degree courses must ensure that theory and research directly informs and supports practice.*
>
> *The Requirements for Social Work Training set out the minimum standards for entry to social work degree courses and for the teaching and assessment that social work students must receive. The new degree will require social workers to demonstrate their practical application of skills and knowledge and their ability to solve problems and provide hope for people relying on social services for support.*
>
> (Jacqui Smith, 2002)

This book provides practical guidance in relation to sensory issues. This is done by highlighting the benefits of students using a combination of theory, legislation and skills in order for them to have a framework upon which to build their practice.

This book aims to enable anyone working with someone with a sensory need to be prepared and competent to undertake effective assessment. This is made possible by exploration of various aspects of sensory need including Deaf/deafness, visual impairment and deafblindness and highlights that small interventions in our practice can have effective outcomes. The importance of multi-agency working is highlighted, as often specialist input enhances the assessment outcome, and subsequently creative service provision for the service user.

This book also aims to meet subject skills identified in the Quality Assurance Agency academic benchmark criteria for social work. These include understanding sensory awareness issues in relation to social work and developing analytical and reflective skills to use within our practice. To enable students to begin or to raise existing sensory awareness this book has explored topics such as:

- the meaning of sensory need (Chapter 1);
- the importance of appropriate communication (Chapter 2);
- how sensory issues have been perceived within the medical and social models and the impact on social work (Chapter 3);
- the importance of adherence to anti-discriminatory practice (Chapter 3);
- the usefulness of theoretical tools in social work practice, e.g. ethical theoretical concepts of deontology and utilitarianism (Chapter 4);

- understanding attachment, resilience, vulnerability and cultural awareness in relation to sensory need (Chapter 5);

- mental health issues and sensory need (Chapter 6).

Application of guidance within this book will assist students to acquire effective communication skills which meet individual need, skills in working with others, and reflective skills in personal and professional development.

While in essence the book focuses on sensory issues, it will also enable students to focus on aspects that are at the core of achieving a social work degree such as GSCC codes of practice, National Occupational Standard Key Roles (NOS), theoretical application, legislation, critical thinking and the essentiality of cultural awareness and anti-discriminatory practice.

Book structure

This book consists of six chapters and endeavours to cover all aspects of sensory awareness in relation to Deaf/deafness, visual impairment and deafblindness in adults and children. The book consistently highlights the need to treat each person as an individual as no two people will experience identical sensory needs. All chapters begin with highlighting the importance of adherence to the National Occupational Standard key roles and General Social Care Council (GSCC) codes of practice which state clearly that operational process skills are central to competence. Throughout the book case studies (vignettes) and activities are used to encourage critical reflection and analysis.

Chapter 1 discusses definitions of sensory needs. This chapter outlines what constitutes sensory need and subsequently sets the scene for the other chapters of the book.

Chapter 2 provides an overview of communication methods for people with sensory need. This useful chapter explores a range of communication methods which include British Sign Language, deafblind alphabet and Braille to name a few. This chapter also provides communication tips and technical awareness for social workers and care managers who may find themselves working with someone who has a sensory need.

Chapter 3 focuses on discrimination faced by people who experience sensory need. As stereotyping has continued into modern society, it is imperative that discrimination is challenged and your practice is anti-discriminatory. As this chapter progresses, it highlights the importance of understanding legislation and theoretical concepts such as the medical and social models of disability and Thompson's (2006) PCS model, as this will influence our practice and thus impact our intervention.

Chapters 4 and 5 explore sensory need within adult and children's services respectively. Chapter 4 explores how sensory need can increase risk of vulnerability, isolation and depression and looks at the concepts of finite and infinite loss with regard to bereavement and loss. The chapter also explores the ethical concepts of deontology and utilitarianism and its application to sensory need. This chapter is also useful for exploration of adult assessment frameworks. Chapter 5 explores using genograms, culturegrams and ecomaps, which are really useful in capturing the essence of working with families in a symbolic/pictorial approach. The chapter also looks at assessment frameworks from a child and family setting.

Chapter 6 focuses on sensory need and mental health. In this chapter students are introduced to key terminology used and are shown how theoretical models have influenced the language used. This chapter explains what is meant by a mental health problem and explores the main forms of mental health problems while incorporating theoretical and legislative application.

All six chapters are aimed at enhancing sensory knowledge and subsequently awareness. However, they also aim to enhance student skills in relation to understanding application of theory to practice. All chapters endeavour to enable students to see the significance of not just the academic process of learning theory, legislation and codes of practice, but how they really apply when practising in social care. Most students find grasping theory difficult, but once learned it is a valuable asset as it underpins practice and provides a valuable framework upon which to start planning intervention. As you become more familiar with different theoretical models and concepts, you may find you begin with one, and then change to another or be eclectic and use a combination. This is good practice as theoretical application is just like people: individual.

Finally the glossary explains any sensory technical terms that are used throughout the book.

Learning features

The book is interactive. You are encouraged to work through the book as an active participant, taking responsibility for your learning, in order to increase your knowledge, understanding and ability to apply this learning to practice. You will be expected to reflect creatively on how immediate learning needs can be met in the area of sensory awareness and how your professional learning can be developed in your future career.

Case studies throughout the book will help you to examine theories and models for social work practice. We have devised activities that require you to reflect on experiences, situations and events and help you to review and summarise learning undertaken. In this way your knowledge will become deeply embedded as part of your development. When you come to practice learning in an agency, the work and reflection undertaken here will help you to improve and hone your skills and knowledge.

This book will introduce knowledge and learning activities for you as a student social worker about the central processes relating to issues of daily practice in all areas of the discipline. At the end of each chapter there are suggestions for further reading. These are to encourage you to carry out personal research which can contribute to supporting and informing your practice.

Skills base

Although this book will not make you a sensory specialist overnight, it will equip you with awareness to work with people who have sensory needs while you are exploring what other resources are available. It may be that in the area in which you work, sensory resources are more limited than in other areas. The aim of this book is to raise sensory awareness and enable all workers to notice if a person has a sensory need and act upon their observations. Not all sensory need is obvious, as not everyone will use a visual language such as British Sign Language (Deaf), use a white symbol cane (visual impairment/blindness) or wear a hearing aid (Deaf/deaf). It may be that a person has isolated themselves as they have found it just too hard to communicate and explain their predicament. Sensory awareness skills in the social care profession are essential as technological and medical advancements develop and as more people live longer and therefore more people experience sensory need. Therefore, all social care workers and professionals should be encouraged to read this book, to enable them to recall it to mind should they find themselves working with someone with sensory need.

Professional development and reflective practice

Great emphasis is placed on developing skills of reflection about, in and on practice. This has been [or: evolved] developed over many years in social work. It is important also that you reflect prior to practice, if indeed social work is your goal. This book will assist you in developing a questioning approach that looks in a critical way at your thoughts, experiences and practice and seeks to heighten your skills in refining your practice as a result of these deliberations. Reflection is central to good social work practice, but only if action results from that reflection.

Reflecting about, in and on your practice is not only important during your education to become a social worker; it is considered key to continued professional development. As we move to a profession that acknowledges lifelong learning as a way of keeping up to date, ensuring that research informs practice and in honing skills and values for practice, it is important to begin the process at the outset of your development. As highlighted earlier, the importance of professional development is clearly shown by its inclusion in the National Occupational Standards; reflected in the GSCC Code of Practice for Employees and echoed in the children's workforce development programmes implemented for newly qualified social workers (NQSWs) and social workers on the early professional development programme (EPD).

Chapter 1

What are sensory needs?

Introduction

In this chapter, we will discuss definitions of sensory needs and what actually constitutes a sensory need and this will set the scene for the remainder of the book. While sensory need incorporates various facets of sensory loss, for the purpose of this book we will be focusing on sensory need in terms of Deaf/deafness, visual impairment and deafblindness. We will explore definitions for visual impairment, deafblindness, deafness including big 'D' deafness (which takes a politicised stance), small 'd' deaf (profoundly deaf, but more often speech used instead of BSL), hard of hearing and deafened. We will consider the registration process and what this means for a person with sensory needs. Within the field of sensory practice, equipment plays a significant role so we will be looking at equipment and technology that can contribute to empowering a person with sensory requirements. The role of linking theory to practice will also be introduced, as will the significance of service user perspectives/involvement and legislation.

What are sensory needs?

'Sensory' is defined as a *sensation of the senses* (Thompson, 1996). This term is based on the Latin *sentire sens,* literally meaning 'to feel'. Needs are defined as *circumstances requiring some form of action; necessity* (Thompson, 1996). Therefore it could be argued that a sensory need is a circumstance which necessitates action in relation to the senses. This could mean that a sensory need is a need for information, advice and/or provision of services in relation to a sensory issue. This could be in connection with hearing and/or sight issues, touch (perhaps because of stroke), taste (dysgeusia) or smell (anosmia). However, as highlighted earlier, for the purpose of this book we will be focusing on sensory needs in terms of deafness/Deafness, hearing impairment, visual impairment and deafblindness.

It could be argued that sensory needs can vary not only medically but also according to how individuals perceive themselves. To illustrate, we will consider two case studies of individuals who are both profoundly deaf/Deaf.

CASE STUDY

Didier was a successful foreign journalist. After contracting meningococcal infection (meningitis) he subsequently experienced a profound hearing loss. Didier's previous world had revolved around being able to hear and receive audible information at a quick pace, interpret the information and act on information received (Shannon and Weaver, 1949). Didier experienced feelings of bereavement, anger, depression and isolation and felt disabled by his hearing loss as his ability to function as a hearing person diminished overnight.

A person in Didier's situation who has acquired deafness as a result of illness, accident, trauma or infection would most likely consider themselves to have sensory loss (Hearing Concern, 2007). People in this situation are often referred to as small 'd' deaf. However, some 'Deaf' people take a politicised stand on deafness and do not consider themselves to have a sensory loss.

CASE STUDY

Vincenta was born profoundly 'Deaf' to parents who were also profoundly culturally Deaf. Vincenta's first language was British Sign Language, which her parents taught her from an early age. Vincenta did not consider herself to be disabled. She was proud to be part of the Deaf community which was rich in culture and history.

Culturally 'Deaf' people are often referred to as 'D' Deaf. Sacks (1991) describes Deaf people who have been part of a Deaf community as a linguistic minority with their own culture and history. The Royal National Institute for Deaf People (2001) was prominent in campaigns to establish British Sign Language (BSL) as an official language in a similar way to Welsh. The government concluded that 'D' Deaf people who considered themselves to be a linguistic minority were justified in their argument and in 2001, British Sign Language was recognised as an official language. Organisations such as the Royal National Institute for Deaf People (RNID) ensure people are well informed about their rights and how to use legislation such as the Disability Discrimination Act 1995 to promote change. An example of this is that all public information is now available in BSL (RNID, 2007). Later in the book, the politicised stance on Deafness will be explored further.

Key definitions

This section aims to clarify sensory definitions for:

- deafness and hearing impairment;
- visual impairment;
- deafblindness.

Deafness and hearing impairment

The World Health Organisation (WHO) defines deafness in terms of the average hearing threshold at three frequencies: 500Hz, 1KHz, and 2KHz. This is the case because these three frequencies cover the main speech spectrum of 300–3000 Hz. Deafness is often used to describe a profound loss in one or both ears and hearing impairment is a loose term used to describe a loss of hearing in one or both ears (World Health Organisation, 2009). There are two types of hearing impairment depending on where the hearing loss occurs. Conductive hearing loss often occurs in the outer or middle ear and can be medically or surgically treatable. Sensorineural hearing loss is usually as a result of a problem in the inner ear. Sensorineural loss can often be permanent and frequently occurs as a result of exposure to excessive/prolonged noise or advancing years. A hearing aid may be useful to someone with sensorineural hearing loss. Hearing loss can be mild, moderate or profound. People can experience deafness or hearing impairment at any time in their lives. Some people are born deaf/Deaf/hearing impaired, otherwise known as congenital deafness, and other people acquire it. Acquisition of deafness/hearing impairment can be at any time throughout life for a whole host of reasons, as highlighted in the case study of Didier.

Deafness/hearing impairment are referred to in different ways:

- big 'D' Deaf;
- small 'd' deaf;
- hard of hearing;
- deafened.

Deafness/hearing impairment is as unique and individual as the person themselves. While two people may be deaf/hearing impaired, they may perceive their deafness/hearing impairment, their method of communication and their social interactions differently.

Within the Deaf/deaf community, there are divided views with regard to deafness being classified as a disability. Someone who has acquired deafness would most likely consider themselves disabled (Hearing Concern, 2007) but 'D' Deaf people take a politicised stand on deafness and do not consider themselves to be disabled (Peters, 2000). A person who is small 'd' deaf would more often communicate using lipreading, residual hearing, speech or hearing aids. However, some deaf people will choose a mixture of communication methods often referred to as 'total communication', which may include British Sign Language, Sign Supported English, simple signs and gestures (see Chapter 2). Big 'D' Deaf people will most likely use British Sign Language.

There are also various genetic disorders that can affect hearing, for example, neurofibromatosis, also known as Bilateral Acoustic NF (BAN). This largely genetic disorder often manifests the first symptoms in the early teens or early twenties.

A person who is deafened may have become deafened by exposure to loud music, heavy machinery or prolonged loud noise (sensorineural). When we use the expression that noise is 'deafening', this can literally mean that the noise is so loud that abnormalities occur in the hair cells of the organ of Corti in the cochlea and prevent sound being transmitted.

The time of life in which a person experiences deafness/hearing impairment can affect their social interactions, education, access to employment, relationships and so on. For a person who has previously experienced hearing, the loss of this sense can be devastating. However, as highlighted, this is not the case in all areas of Deafness.

Visual impairment

According to the World Health Organisation, blindness is the inability to see due to physiological or neurological factors (WHO, 2009). Previously people with visual impairment/sight difficulties were referred to as 'blind' and 'partially sighted'; now the terms used are 'sight impaired' and 'severely sight impaired'. While these changes have been made, many people still refer to people as blind and partially sighted, so we will be using both terms throughout this book. Blindness can incorporate various aspects of blindness, for example, total blindness, which is the complete lack of form and visual light perception and therefore clinically recorded as 'NLP', which literally stands for 'no light perception'. Blindness is also often used to describe severe visual impairment with residual vision. People described as having 'light perception' only have the sight ability to differentiate light from dark. People who have 'light projection' are able to locate the general direction of a light source. 'Peripheral blindness' is due to a lesion in the optical apparatus peripheral to the optical cortex, including lesions in the optic chiasma, optic nerve, retina, anterior and posterior chambers, lens and cornea. The term 'blindness' may indicate a total loss of vision or may be used to describe certain visual limitations, e.g. colour-blindness (tritanopia).

There are numerous causes of visual impairment. However, the primary causes of chronic blindness include cataract, glaucoma, age-related macular degeneration (AMD), corneal opacities, diabetic retinopathy and trachoma. As people are living longer, age-related blindness is increasing, as is blindness caused by uncontrolled diabetes. Additionally, there is a host of eye conditions associated with children, for example, conditions caused by vitamin A deficiency. A percentage of eye conditions can be treated or controlled but some eye conditions are permanent. Where visual impairment is permanent, statutory support is offered.

A significant aspect of support for an individual who is sight impaired or severely sight impaired is that of registration. We will look at the registration process and the legislation that supports it later in this chapter.

Deafblindness

The term 'deafblind' usually refers to children and adults who have both a hearing and vision impairment. This combination of sensory loss is often described in various terminological formats, including:

- deafblindness (DB);
- dual sensory loss (DSL);
- multi-sensory impairment (MSI).

Throughout this book you will see all three terms used. However, DSL is more likely to be used in a clinical context (Bernstein, 2007); deafblindness is more likely to be used by service users experiencing sensory needs (SENSE, 2006); and MSI is more likely to be used in educational settings by the Department for Children, Schools and Families (DCFS), School Census and Early Support. Terminological clarity is significant because not everyone understands the meanings conveyed by the terminology. For example, MSI could indicate a loss of a number of senses, not just sight and sound; DSL could imply that the senses involved were not just vision and hearing but could be a loss of any two senses, possibly taste (dysgeusia) and smell (anosmia). The term 'deafblind' is most likely to be the one that the wider audience will understand as meaning a person who has sight and hearing difficulties. SENSE and Deafblind UK, organisations specialising in issues relating to deafblindness, use the term deafblind in much of their literature. However, it is important to remember that while the term deafblind may imply that the person is profoundly deaf and profoundly blind, sight and vision loss varies according to each individual.

While there is a variety of medical conditions in which people experience deafblindness, advancing years is the major cause for deafblindness. Other conditions include Usher syndrome, which is characterised by congenital hearing loss, deterioration of vision due to retinitis pigmentosa and vestibular difficulties. There are three types of usher.

Usher Type 1
People with Type 1 are profoundly deaf from birth, with poor balance. The progressive eye condition, retinitis pigmentosa (RP for short), can be noticeable before the age of 10.

Usher Type 2
People with Type 2 have a partial to severe hearing loss from birth. Their balance is normal. The RP is usually, but not always, noticeable before the age of 20.

Usher Type 3
This is the rarest type of Usher syndrome in the UK. People with Type 3 have normal sight and either normal or partial hearing at birth. The deterioration of the hearing and the diagnosis of the RP commonly happen at roughly the same time, either in adulthood or, occasionally, in children or teenagers. Balance can become affected over time. (Information from SENSE, 2009)

CHARGE is another condition which affects children, young people and adults and was identified in 1979. The name CHARGE is an acronym of some of the features thought to manifest themselves in the condition; however, research is still ongoing on this matter (SENSE, 2009).

Definition

Guidance issued under the Local Authority Social Services Act 1970 under Section 7 defines persons as being deafblind if they have a severe degree of combined visual and auditory impairment resulting in problems with communication, information and mobility. The Act defines the four main groups of deafblind people as: people born deafblind; people born deaf/Deaf and who later lose vision; people born blind; and who lose hearing and people with acquired deafblindness. SENSE, a voluntary organisation working with people who are deafblind, defines deafblindness as the combined loss of hearing and sight (SENSE, 2006). They describe the impact of the combined loss as, *not just a deaf person who cannot see or a blind person who cannot hear. The two impairments impact on each other and multiply the total effect* (SENSE, 2006, p3). SENSE uses the analogy that *if you think of deafness as the colour yellow and blindness as the colour blue, when you mix the two together you don't get yellow-blue but a completely different colour – green* (SENSE, 2006, p3). If you lose your sight you have your hearing to rely on, if you lose your hearing you have your sight to rely on, but when you lose both you have neither sense to rely on and the complexity of the multi-sensory loss causes further complexities.

Xiomar needs to go to the shops for some milk. There is a busy road between his home and the shop. This presents difficulties for Xiomar because he is deafblind. If Xiomar were blind he could still hear the beep of a pedestrian crossing in order to cross safely. If he were deaf/ Deaf he could see the flashing green man. However, Xiomar is deafblind and cannot use either of the methods a blind or deaf/Deaf person could use to cross the road safely.

ACTIVITY *1.1*

Draw on your imagination or previous knowledge you have of working with people who are deafblind and work out a safe intervention for Xiomar to cross the road.

Comment

As you may have concluded, Xiomar can neither hear the beep of a pedestrian crossing nor see the flashing green man. The loss of both senses creates unique complexities and the result of deafblindness is that you have neither sense to rely on and thus things other people take for granted pose a significant risk (SENSE, 2007). On some pedestrian crossings there may be a tactile signal in the form of a small round metal knob at the base of the control box that activates when the traffic lights change and indicates it is safe to cross. However, this device is not available at all pedestrian crossings and if available does not always function appropriately.

Deafblindness is significantly impacted by the time of life in which a person became deafblind. If a person was able to see and hear earlier in their life and later acquired deafblindness, it could mean that they had access to acquire speech and language skills, build a career and relationships. For children who are deafblind from birth and as such deprived of accidental learning, this may mean that speech and language acquisition, social skills, educational access and so on, are far more restricted and sometimes deafblind children are limited to what they can taste, touch and smell.

Registration

Visually impaired people

The National Assistance Act 1948 outlines the following points.

- A person can be registered blind if they are so blind that they cannot do any work for which eyesight is essential.

- A person can be registered as blind if their visual acuity is 3/60 or worse or 6/60 if their field of vision is very restricted.

- There is no legal definition of partial sight.

- A person may be certified as partially sighted if they are not blind within the meaning of the 1948 Act but are substantially and permanently handicapped by defective vision, caused by congenital defect or illness or injury.

- Registration document BD8 (now called Certificate of Visual Impairment – CVI)

Registration to identify a person as partially sighted or severely partially sighted is carried out by the ophthalmic consultant; however, the original referral needs to be via the GP.

Deafblind people

While there is currently no formal registration for deafblind children and adults, in March 2001 the government issued statutory guidance entitled *Social Care for Deafblind Children and Adults* under section 7 of the Local Authority and Social Services Act 1970. The guidance in this circular is relevant to all local social services and educational staff and requires specific actions to be taken such as identifying and keeping records on deafblind people in catchment areas (DoH, 2001). This guidance meant that local authorities had to:

- identify, make contact with and keep a record of deafblind people;

- provide assessments carried out by a specifically trained person/team;

- provide appropriate services;

- provide one-to-one support (communicator guides) who provide assistance with correspondence, telephone calls, reading newspapers, escorting on shopping trips, appointments (such as hospital, GP, hairdresser), social engagements, cultural or recreational activities or conversations at home to relieve isolation and information in accessible formats.

- ensure that senior management have overall responsibility.

While this document is guidance, not legislation, if local authorities failed to adhere to this guidance they could be subject to judicial review.

As the lead agency responsible for safeguarding and promoting the welfare of vulnerable children and adults, local authorities undertake to work in partnership with other public agencies, the independent and voluntary sectors and service users to develop inter-agency policies and practices to protect vulnerable adults from abuse in all settings. Local authorities have statutory responsibilities to provide a wide range of care and support for vulnerable children and adults.

Deaf people

There is no specific legislation that covers only Deaf, deaf, deafened or hard of hearing people. Rather there is a number of pieces of legislation that address hearing needs and deafness as a disability.

Legislation available to an individual with a disability includes the following.

- Disability Discrimination Act 1995/2005.
- Chronically Sick and Disabled Act 1970 – this Act may (permissive power) be used to provide practical assistance to a person with sensory needs. This could be in the form of equipment and adaptation provision (depending on local authority procedures, protocols and service delivery).
- Disability Rights Commission Act 1999.
- Community Care (Direct Payments) Act 1996.
- National Health Service and Community Care Act 1990, Section 47 Duty to assess.
- Human Rights Act 1998.
- Carers and Disabled Children Act 2000.

For further information on legislation see Office of Public Sector Information, available at www.opsi.gov.uk/acts.

An important point is that there is a distinction between mandatory and permissive powers. Mandatory means compulsory while permissive means 'may'. Johns (2005) highlights that the law *rarely makes the provision of specific services as such mandatory, preferring to make provision of information about services compulsory* (2005, p18). An example of this is the Chronically Sick and Disabled Act 1970. Permissive powers are important to local authorities as they have discretion at a local level. If they act outside of their jurisdiction, they are acting *ultra vires* or beyond powers (Johns, 2005).

Equipment and services

Equipment can be a major factor in empowerment, independence and well-being. A simple piece of equipment can be life changing. In this section we will be exploring the range of equipment available to deaf, blind and deafblind people.

Visually impaired people

There is a variety of equipment, environment solutions, human aids (sighted guides), canine aids (guide dogs), guidance and information for people who are sight impaired or severely sight impaired. However, what is used may depend on the level of sight loss, age, other disabilities, confidence, culture and choice. In this section we will briefly look at some of these. For more information contact Royal National Institute for the Blind (www. rnib.org.uk) and the local authority sensory services team Visual Impairment Rehabilitation Worker. This may be in-house or contracted out to a voluntary organisation or charity; your local authority should be able to advise.

There is an assortment of canes used by people with visual difficulties.

- Symbol cane – not made to support a person's body weight. This cane is like a badge or sign to show others that the person is blind or visually impaired. This would most likely be used by someone with some residual vision.

- Guide cane – sturdier than a symbol cane. A guide cane should always point to the floor and can be used in a diagonal position across the lower part of the body for protection or using a scanning technique to check for kerbs and steps. The cane should reach just above waist level when the user is standing upright with the tip of the cane touching the ground between their legs. Guide canes are not to be used for supporting a person's body weight (RNIB, 2007).

- Long cane – designed primarily as a mobility tool used to detect objects in the path of a user. Cane length depends upon the height of a user, and traditionally extends from the floor to the user's sternum. There can be a roller on the tip of the cane. The user needs to be trained in using this cane. This would most likely be used by someone with little or no sight.

- White walking sticks are often issued to people who used a walking stick previously and require some support for walking.

CASE STUDY

Kueng is registered blind. Kueng travels to work by bus every day and uses his symbol cane to highlight to the bus driver and passengers that he is blind/severely partially sighted. This means that the driver will allow time for Kueng to get on and off the bus. Kueng works near a busy shopping centre, so once again he uses his cane to alert others to his blindness. When Kueng arrives at work he folds the cane up and continues with his work.

Guide dogs are another aid that blind and visually impaired people use to enable them to feel safe. For example with a guide dog, a visually impaired/blind person can tell where the road begins and the pavement ends (www.gdba.org.uk).

In sensory terms, equipment for visually impaired people is crucial in making the person's home safe and accessible. One of the great inventions for visually impaired people is a tiny self-adhesive piece of polyurethane, smaller than the little fingernail, known as a 'bumpon'. Bumpons are uncomplicated and tactile. When used on, for example, a cooker the visually impaired/blind person is able to identify the gas/electric mark and have choice and autonomy while remaining safe. Bumpons can be used on anything from a microwave to a mobile phone.

Other equipment or environmental changes that are beneficial for people with a visual impairment include the following.

- Magnifiers, e.g. hand magnifier, dome/bar magnifier, spectacle magnifier and binoculars. Specialist magnifiers can range from 1.5x magnification to 15x magnification (RNIB, 2009).

- Talking equipment, such as watches, clocks and microwaves.

- Braille tactile watches.

- Games – tactile dominoes and large playing cards (RNIB, 2009)

- Lighting can be used to enhance residual vision. Specialist fluorescent lamps have low wattage and provide directional 'daylight'-type lighting which can improve contrast, assisting with near vision to enable detail and text to be sharper. Some lights also have magnifier attachments. Lighting needs to be kept even and potentially unsafe areas such as stairs, kitchens and bathrooms need to be well lit.

- Colour contrast – this can be used when writing a letter (i.e. black text on yellow paper); to contrasting the edge of stairs or steps (black and yellow tape and painting the step black with a yellow edge) or even around door frames (walls one colour, door frames contrasting). Contrast can also be used on a computer keyboard.

- Telephones, e.g. BT Big Button.

- Non-slip surfaces for flooring, place mats and coasters.

- Mobile phone – the Owasys 22C is a talking phone that is designed specifically for blind and partially sighted people. The phone has easy-to-find and tactile keypad buttons, absence of a screen, built speech facility and a computerised voice which talks through the phone's functions (RNIB, 2009).

- Computer software – JAWS is screen-reading software for Windows programmes. It enables web browsing, use of email, read and write documents, use of spreadsheets, databases and other programmes. Magic 10.5 is a screen magnifier with a colour-coded user interface. Also available is Braille/Moon (a series of raised dots/symbols to be translated using touch) display to access all the information available to sighted people (for more information see www.braillemaker.com).

- Audio description (AD) – like a narrator telling a story, audio description is an additional commentary describing body language, expressions and movements. AD gives you information about the things you might not be able to see, meaning that you can keep up with the action (RNIB, 2009).

The local visual impairment rehabilitation worker may provide sighted guide training. A sighted guide can be used by a visually impaired person to enable them to travel. However, use will depend on the visually impaired person's confidence and competence in travel skills and can be influenced by personal preference, age, culture and additional disabilities. The sighted guide can be used to familiarise the visually impaired person with a new area, such as a hospital or when travelling in busy areas or going on walks. The visually impaired person would most likely use a sighted guide in addition to the appropriate cane for their needs.

CASE STUDY

Abayomi had been visually impaired since the age of 28 years following trauma. Despite having sight difficulties, Abayomi had led an active life and travelled to many places. However, as she advanced in years her health and mobility deteriorated and most of her family had passed away, so she required nursing home care. The nursing home was not deafblind aware and on Thursdays the set menu consisted of white mashed potato, cauliflower and white fish presented on a white plate.

ACTIVITY 1.2

Imagine you are Abayomi. You are visually impaired and your vision is limited. There is no contrast either in the colour of your plate or the food that is placed upon it. How do you think you would manage to eat? Do you think that it would be difficult to work out what is the plate and what is food? Can you imagine Abayomi being able to eat this compilation of food successfully? Or do you think the plate and the food would merge into one?

Comment

You do not have to be specialist worker to empower the people you work with to maximise residual vision; use of simple techniques and strategies can enhance a visually impaired person's quality of daily living. For example, with the case of Abayomi, you could ensure the plate was a brighter colour or have a darker contrast around the edge of the plate, to maximise the visibility of the food. The food could be of contrasting colours, for example if the mashed potato is white, present it with carrots or broccoli. These simple changes could empower a visually impaired person and enable them to have more dignity and control in their lives.

Deaf/deaf

The range of equipment used by Deaf/deaf/hard of hearing and deafened people is quite extensive. Installation of a simple piece of equipment can have a far-reaching impact on the individual. This can range from safeguarding, for example use of a baby alarm to ensure a parent carer is alerted to a crying baby to prevention of isolation as in the case of telephone or doorbell alert. In this section, we will be exploring some of the equipment, human aids and services available for Deaf/deaf/hearing impaired people.

- Vibrating pager system, clocks, watches, baby alarms – the pager system is a small device that someone can put in their pocket or clip to a belt. When a signal is received from a sensor such as a doorbell, baby alarm or smoke alarm, the pager activates by vibrating. A visual symbol is produced for each alert. For people who are blind/partially sighted or deafblind there is a vibration facility with different vibration patterns for each alert.

- Visual alert systems, e.g. visual flashing doorbells, visual flashing smoke alarms.

- Text phones, e.g. Minicom, or combined voice and text phone, e.g. Uniphone.

- Loop – for use with a hearing aid. The hearing aid is switched to the 'T' position to enable sound to be amplified directly from the technological appliance to the hearing aid.

- MiniTech/Crescendo portable listener – this can be used to amplify sound on a one-to-one basis or for use to enhance television sound. Infrared TV listeners are also available. These are invaluable if provided to an elderly or frail person as there are no trailing wires.

- Television – subtitles, caption reader (look out for this on DVDs as it means subtitles are available).

- Portable telephone amplifiers can be connected to a telephone. Alternatively, telephones with inductive couplers (for use with hearing aid) or amplified telephones (for people who do not wear hearing aids) are available.

- Fax machine.

For further information regarding equipment, see RNID website (www.rnid.org.uk).

An invaluable service worth knowing about is the National Deaf Children Society (NDCS) Blue Peter technology loan service. This is a free UK-wide loan service which enables deaf/ Deaf children to try out equipment in their own school and home. The advantage of this service is that it's a 'try before you buy' facility. The equipment can be tried out and if suit-able either purchased privately or requested from the local authority (children, families and education). The NDCS also have useful booklets available such as *Technology at home*, which explains about the variety of equipment and how to purchase it, and *Radio aids, an introductory guide,* which explains about the usefulness of radio aids and different models available. The NDCS also has a useful website which can provide guidance to families and professionals (www.ndcs.org.uk).

Hearing Dogs for Deaf People (www.hearingdogs.org.uk) is a registered charity. Hearing dogs are primarily for people with a severe or profound hearing loss. They respond to everyday sounds within the home or/and workplace. The dogs communicate by touch and then lead to the source of sound, thus providing the deaf person with greater inde-pendence, confidence and awareness of their environment. Hearing dogs can also offer companionship and security which promotes independence and avoids isolation. While a referral can be made, the organisation carries out its own assessments.

Additionally, there is the use of interpreters and various environmental changes that could be made to enhance residual hearing and these will be explored further in Chapter 2.

Deafblind

Deafblind people may be able to utilise any of the canes that a visually impaired person uses, but instead of the cane being white (to indicate the person is visually impaired), it would be red and white to indicate the person is deafblind.

A deafblind person can also utilise a combination of the equipment, techniques or envi-ronmental changes available for a visually impaired or Deaf/deaf person. The use of equipment, techniques and environmental changes will depend on the level of sight loss in relation to the level of hearing loss. Some people will have greater vision than hearing and vice versa, therefore technological and environmental requirements will be unique to the individual. However, one aspect that needs to be emphasised is that DSL/ DB/MSI leads to greater sensory complexity, thus practice needs to be particularly sensitive, empathic and unique.

Communicator guides

A communicator guide is a person trained to provide a one-to-one enabling service to deafblind adults. A communicator guide would not normally provide the developmental support that an intervenor would provide (see below). The tasks that communicator guides carry out will fluctuate depending on the individual deafblind person, their level of residual hearing and vision and the communication skills they have acquired.

Communicator guides are human facilitators. Their work focuses on:

- communication;
- information;
- access;
- mobility.

A typical role of a communicator guide may involve assisting with correspondence, telephone calls, reading newspapers, escorting on a shopping trip, appointments (such as hospital, GP, hairdresser) social engagements, cultural or recreational activities or conversation at home to relieve isolation. A communicator guide will assist with a whole range of jobs, from everyday tasks to special events. Assistance in connection with these jobs must be as a direct result of a person's deafblindness.

Communicator guides are not home care workers. Communicator guides provide an enablement service that promotes independence, autonomy and reduction of social isolation. The communication guide service is specialist and unique and should not be used as a replacement for other social services or health service provision (SENSE, 2007).

While in some areas this service may be provided to young people, this service can most likely be accessed through the local authority adults' sensory service or the local authority adults' physical disability team. If this is unavailable, SENSE or Deafblind UK may be able to provide guidance.

Intervenors

An intervenor would most likely provide support for children and young people aged birth–19 years who are severely or profoundly deafblind/MSI. The intervenor would be a human aid to communication; assist the child in accessing information; empower the child or young person to have independent mobility; assist them in interpreting the world and support their learning process. The intervenor's role would also incorporate working with other professionals (e.g. specialist teaching services for MSI children and young people, social workers, communicator guides), working in partnership with the parents, developing the inclusion of the child or young people in family life, educational settings and community activities. This service can most likely be accessed through either the local Education Specialist Teaching Service, the Disabled Children's Service or the Sensory Service. However, if this is unavailable, as with the communication guide service, SENSE or Deafblind UK may be able to provide guidance.

Linking theory to practice

The importance of use of theoretical frameworks and individual tailor-made assessment when assessing people with sensory needs cannot be emphasised enough. Theoretical frameworks continually underpin the assessment process and subsequent interventions we make. Whether we are working in a child and family setting, adult service provision or mental health services you will find there will always be a need for theory to influence and underpin your practice. Often students find linking theory to practice a difficult task. To illustrate how naturally and easily it can be done, let's explore the case study of Abdikarim.

CASE STUDY

Abdikarim is 19 years old and moved from Somali as a result of the civil war. He is sight impaired, has a mild hearing loss and has severe mobility difficulties following trauma sustained during the conflict. Abdikarim finds it difficult to communicate as he has sensory needs and his first language is Somali. Abdikarim attends the local college in a bid to learn English, but the fact he has severe sensory and physical impairments hinders his progress. Abdikarim presents as having low self-esteem, is isolated and uncommunicative.

Abdikarim's situation is a complex one. Not only does he have sensory needs, but also cultural, social, psychological, physical, and communicative needs.

ACTIVITY 1.3

You are Abdikarim's care manager; what do you think may be a good starting point in your intervention with him? Take into account Abdikarim's individual, personal needs.

Comment

Your assessment may have concluded that further exploration of Abdikarim's cultural and social needs are required to raise his self-esteem. You may have empowered Abdikarim to explore this himself by encouraging him to search the internet for local Somali community groups. Access to his cultural heritage may empower Abdikarim. Additionally, it may also enable him to communicate in his first language, which may prevent isolation and empower him to share feelings and experiences and raise his self-esteem.

Without realising it, your intervention was probably influenced by theory. We often use theoretical influences in everyday problem-solving. For example, encouraging Abdikarim to research local community groups is setting him a meaningful but achievable task. Therefore this method of practice intervention could be described as task-centred (Reid, 1977). The task-centred approach grew out of Reid and Shyne's (1969) work on short-

and long-term intervention comparison and Studt's work on structured intervention (Reid, 1977, p1). Task-centred practice focuses on enabling service users to make small, meaningful changes in their lives, rather than focusing on radical change (Healy, 2005). When practising in a task-centred way it is essential to be clear on the purpose of the task, making it achievable. The success that the service user can feel from being empowered to achieve can create a desire for further achievement and have a constructive impact on future change in one's life.

Another theoretical approach that could have influenced your practice intervention with Abdikarim could have been psychodynamic theory, as it has been argued that *psychodynamic theory offers a useful understanding of human emotions, interactions and internal responses to the outside world* (Payne, 2005, p148). The most well-known theorist, Sigmund Freud, explained human behaviour and psychological problems by exploring stages of early childhood experiences (Crawford and Walker, 2004, p8). Psychodynamic approaches have been very influential in social work and there is current interest in how it can inform frontline social work practice (Bower, 2005). Psychodynamic theory could be used in intervention to explore what it was like for Abdikarim as a child, the impact of the trauma he has experienced and what it felt like for him moving to a different country where the lifestyle and language differ so greatly.

From being a dominant framework in social work during the 1940s and 1950s, psychodynamic theory came under attack in the 1960s and 1970s from ideological and empirical critiques. Healy (2005) highlights a number of studies that were carried out to ascertain if long-term psychodynamic case work had greater effectiveness than short-term interventions (Reid and Shyne, 1969; Reid and Epstein, 1972; Reid, 1985). The consensus at that time was that long-term psychodynamic casework did not demonstrate greater effectiveness than shorter interventions (Healy, 2005). More recently, brief solution-focused therapy (De Shazer, 1985) is an innovative theory that challenged the traditional psychodynamic approach and looked at theoretical input from a brief intervention perspective.

It has been suggested that brief solution focused therapy (De Shazer, 1985) and the strengths perspective (Healy, 2005) have similarities. For example, both recognise and focus on:

- strengths that a service user has to solve problems, not their areas for development;
- service user and service provider work in partnership as part of a mutual learning process;
- the fact that the problem is the problem, not that the person is the problem;
- positive future solutions rather that excavating the past (Healy, 2005).

Critical reflection on use of theory to underpin practice suggests that whichever theory we use there is a possibility of inter-theoretical influence. For example, crisis intervention (Roberts, 2000) uses elements of ego psychology from a psychodynamic perspective with more recent developments including cognitive therapy. Similarly, crisis intervention work has influenced task-centred work (Payne, 2005); task-centred work has links with the behavioural approach (Howe, 1987), for example in the use of contracts with service users and MacNeil and Stewart (2000, p241) suggest that *task-centred practice can help to formulate plans for actions in crisis work.*

At first you may feel unsure about which theory to use in practice. You may begin with one theoretical concept and then change your approach as you get to know the person or client group you are working with. This is where the role of evidence and information collation is important when choosing theories for practice. For example, it is important to discover what works within your practice and what works to meet the service user's needs (Walker, Crawford and Parker, 2008). It is only by collating the evidence that you can really get to know the strengths and limitations of the theoretical applications applied to your case work. The evidence and information you collate may be influenced by your own social work values, personal research or governmental policies and procedures. We have discussed how one theory may be influenced by other factors however, as repeatedly highlighted, it is essential that each situation is individually addressed with the service user's individual needs in mind.

The important aspect of applying theory in our practice is to recognise that it is a helpful tool to assist us in considering a plan of intervention. Dealing with human complexities can often leave us as social workers and care managers wondering what the best course of action will be. Using theory to underpin our practice will assist us in making decisions that are in the best interest of the service user, while balancing risk (Parrott, 2007). However, we do not have to be fixed on a single theory, for example cognitive development, ecological development or behaviourism as drawing upon multiple theoretical perspectives can also be beneficial. We may set out with one theory in mind, but as the assessment progresses it may be necessary to critically reflect on the theoretical concept we are considering and explore other options, as highlighted in the case of Abdikarim.

As we have discussed, reflection is an essential tool for social workers and care managers to acquire. This is because reflection generates lots of thoughts, ideas and feelings which in turn influence our learning and development (Brown and Rutter, 2006). Schön (1987) highlights how exploration of these reflections is part of our personal professional development. So while it is essential to understand what is meant by psychodynamic theory or solution-focused theory, it is not until you can actually see how this can apply in your practice that theory becomes a useful and fundamental basis for you to begin your intervention. Thinking on the concept of critical reflection (Brown and Rutter, 2006), let's explore the aspect of professional and service user perspective.

Professional and service user perspective

ACTIVITY *1.4*

To begin, critically reflect on an experience you personally have of working with a service user. This could be in one of your placements or in a role in which you have worked voluntarily, privately or personally. Do you think that the service user's perspectives were valid? Did you listen to what they had to say? Did you incorporate their wishes, thoughts and feelings into your assessment? What do you think you could have been done differently?

Comment

The British Council of Disabled People (BCODP) has achieved change by articulating demands through formal political channels, carrying out research, organising demonstrations and promoting disability equality training (Oliver and Sapey, 2006). Service user involvement can be invaluable when addressing educational programmes to enlighten staff and professionals of the realities of living with sensory disability and the oppression and discrimination they face daily (Warren, 2007).

The Joseph Rowntree Foundation (2007) research highlighted that service user involvement, challenging oppression, discrimination and inclusion, are vital to promote change.

An example of research into service user involvement was carried out by the Joseph Rowntree Foundation entitled *Person-centred support: What service users and practitioners say* (Glynn et al., 2008). This report asked service users to give their views on what they thought person-centred support incorporated. Historically, disabled people have argued that funding spent should enable service users themselves to have choices and opportunities to live ordinary lives. After all, if disabled people are equal in society this means they need to have choice and control over the support they require to continue with their daily living. The government's personalisation programme, which aims to support people to make choices, be autonomous and be included, will be explored further in Chapter 4.

Within a sensory context service user involvement can prove to be vital, as understanding discrimination and complexities that sensory disabled people experience and working out ways to facilitate change is invaluable to best practice. This area of practice will be explored further in Chapter 3.

CHAPTER SUMMARY

In order to practise effectively when working with people with sensory requirements, it is important to understand the sensory context from which the individual comes. For example, understanding difference and diversity in relation to 'D' Deafness and 'd' deafness is not only essential in effective intervention but imperative to enable the service users' views to be understood and appropriate individualised service to be provided. Another aspect highlighted was the importance of recognising that where there is more than one sensory need, as in the case of deafblindness, sensitivity and empathy are required to address the complexity of need that multiple sensory losses produce.

As you progress through this book, you will be able to further develop your understanding and be guided on ways to incorporate sensory awareness into your social work/care management practice.

FURTHER READING

Payne, M (2005) *Modern social work theory*. Third edition. Basingstoke: Palgrave Macmillan.

This book offers a complete introduction to theories of social work practice. Drawing on literature from across the world, the book traces the origins of social work ideas, how they develop, and assesses their role and value based on scholarly debate and research. Compact and clearly structured, the book breaks down key issues in a way that is easy for students to grasp. A truly innovative way of looking at theoretical concepts and their impact on social work.

Thompson, N (2006) *Anti-discriminatory practice*. Fourth edition. Basingstoke: Palgrave.

Tackling discrimination and oppression in social work and social care is now recognised as a fundamental and essential component of good practice. This important textbook offers students, practitioners, managers and educators a clear and accessible analysis of complexities of this crucial aspect of social work theory and practice. This is an essential book for all who take seriously the importance of equality and social justice as a foundation for good social work practice.

Warren, J (2007) *Service user and carer participation in social work*. Exeter: Learning Matters.

The first text to examine service user involvement and participation across both adult and children's services. It is a clear and useful account of the principles and practice of user involvement, which draws together knowledge from research and the experiences of service users, carers and practitioners. It addresses the skills, knowledge and values that social workers need to be effective and make effective use of case studies to illustrate practice situations.

Chapter 2

Communication methods for people with sensory needs

This chapter will help to meet the following National Occupational Standards.

Key Role 1: Prepare for and work with individuals, families, carers, groups and communities to assess their needs and circumstances.
- Assess needs and options to recommend a course of action.

Key Role 2: Plan, carry out, review and evaluate social work practice, with individuals, families, carers, groups, communities and other professionals.
- Interact with families, carers, groups and communities to achieve change and development and to improve life opportunities.
- Work with groups to promote individual growth, development and independence.

Key Role 5: Manage and be accountable, with supervision and support, for your own social work practice within your organisation.
- Carry out duties using accountable professional judgement and knowledge-based social work practice.
- Monitor and evaluate the effectiveness of your programme of work in meeting the organisational requirements and the needs of individuals, families, carers, groups and communities.

This chapter will also assist you to follow the GSCC (General Social Care Council) Codes of Practice for Social Care Workers.

GSCC Code 1: As a social care worker you must protect the rights and promote the interests of service users and carers.
- Treating each person as an individual.
- Respecting and, where appropriate, promoting the individual views and wishes of both service users and carers.
- Supporting service users' rights to control lives and make informed choices about the services they receive.
- Respecting and maintaining the dignity of the service users and carers.
- Respecting diversity and different culture and values.

GSCC Code 3: As a social care worker, you must promote the independence of service users while protecting them as far as possible from danger or harm.
- Promoting the independence of service users and assisting them to understand and exercise their rights.
- Helping service users and carers to make complaints, taking complaints seriously and responding to them or passing them to the appropriate person (e.g. if an interpreter is not provided or is unsuitable).
- Recognising and using responsibly the power that comes from your work with service users and carers.

continued

GSCC Code 6: As a social care worker, you must be accountable for the quality of your work and take responsibility for maintaining and improving your knowledge and skills.
- Maintaining clear and accurate records as required by procedures established for your work.
- Recognising and respecting roles and expertise of workers from other agencies and working in partnership with them (please note: this is essential when working with specialist voluntary organisations, such as BDA, RNID, SENSE, Deafblind UK and RNIB).
- Undertake relevant training to maintain and improve your knowledge and skills and contributing to the learning and development of others.

Introduction

A requirement of the social work degree programme is that students are able to effectively communicate with children, adults and those with additional or special needs (SCIE, 2004). This chapter will be focusing on the issue of communication for people who experience sensory need. It will explore a range of communication methods used by people with sensory needs, including British Sign Language (BSL), deafblind manual alphabet, lip-speaking and Braille. Alternative communication methods will also be explored such as the use of verbal and non-verbal forms of communication, observation and listening skills (Trevithick, 2005). Additionally, it will provide communication tips and practical guidance social workers can use to maximise residual hearing and vision in practice. The significance of the use of theory will be identified using a range of models and concepts. Critical thinking and effective intervention will be encouraged when analysing the importance of cultural knowledge to ensure anti-discriminatory and anti-oppressive practice. We will briefly explore Trevithick's (2005) and Cooley's (1902) concepts of self-awareness and the impact this will have on good practice. We will identify legislative framework that impacts on service delivery when addressing communication needs in respect of a person with sensory requirements. Finally we will look at human aids to communication and technical equipment and how they contribute to the communication process.

To begin we need to define the meaning of communication. Fiske (1990) defines communication as *social interaction through messages* (1990, p2). Use of the word 'social' is significant because communication could be described as a social activity. Without social interaction, especially when addressing sensory communicative needs, an individual could become isolated. This in turn could contribute to other physical and mental health issues such as depression (Chou and Chi, 2004). This can be illustrated through a case study.

CASE STUDY

Olivia is in her 70s and enjoys participating in over-60s coach trips. Olivia enjoys socialising with other people and learning new information that the guide on the trip conveys. However, over the last few years Olivia's hearing has started to deteriorate and she has found that she could not converse easily with other people on the trips or hear what the guide was saying. Olivia stopped booking the coach trips and became isolated. She became depressed and booked an appointment with her GP. She explained to the GP that the depression had begun when she could no longer go on the coach trips because

continued

CASE STUDY continued

she could not hear well now. The GP explained that he would refer Olivia to an audiologist at the local hospital for a hearing test to see if a hearing aid would be useful. While conversing with Olivia he noticed that she was conversing well with him by paying particular attention to his lips. The GP suggested that she attend lipreading classes. The GP explained to Olivia the concept of lipreading and gave her a leaflet with details of a local course. While waiting for her audiology appointment, Olivia attended the course and not only found that she could read lips, but also met other people in a similar situation to herself. Olivia became empowered, more assertive and made new friends on the course. She could once again attend her coach trips except now she explained to the guide that she has a hearing loss and lipreads. She requests that she sits at the front to read the guide's lips and that people face her when they speak.

This case study illustrates how a simple alteration in communication can prevent isolation, empower, and promote independence. It is important to note, however, that communication is 'person/need specific'. This means that each person with a sensory need will use a communication method that is individual to them. As there are many diverse and different forms of communication we may find that as social workers we need to be open-minded in our use of communication.

ACTIVITY **2.1**

List as many communication methods you can think of that could be used when communicating with a person who has a sensory need. Think specifically of a person who is deaf, Deaf, hard of hearing, deafened, deafblind, partially sighted or blind.

Comment

As explained earlier, communication methods for people with sensory need are diverse and different. You may have listed some of the better known communication methods such as British Sign Language (BSL) or Signed Supported English (SSE). However, next we will explore not only some of the better known sensory communicative methods, but also some of the lesser known ones such as Tadoma, which is a method of communication primarily used by people who are deafblind in which the deafblind person places their thumb on the speaker's lips and their fingers along the speaker's jawline. The middle three fingers often fall along the speaker's cheeks with the little finger picking up the vibrations of the speaker's throat.

Communication methods

- British Sign Language (BSL)
- Signed Supported English (SSE)
- Hands-on Signing
- Makaton
- Deafblind manual alphabet
- Block
- Braille
- Moon
- Bold Print Format

- Tadoma
- Lipspeaking
- Lipreading
- Clear Speech
- Cued Articulation (useful in education)
- Paget Gorman
- Cued Speech
- PECS (Pictorial Exchange Communication System)
- Sign Along

(See glossary for full explanation of each communication method.)

Communication is as unique and individual as the person themselves. While two people may be labelled as being deafblind, it does not mean that they will use the same form of communication. It may depend on if the sight or the hearing was lost first; whether a person was born deaf or born blind, or acquired the sensory loss later in life. A good rule of thumb is never to make assumptions about a person's communicative method; always ask them their preferred method of communication and be prepared to be flexible in your own approach.

ACTIVITY 2.2

Look at the following case studies for Richard and James. Technically they are both deaf-blind. Critically reflect on the sensory need each one experiences and their preferred communication method.

CASE STUDY

Richard

Richard was born blind. He could hear until he was 65 then his hearing started to deteriorate. Richard communicated most of his life using clear speech. As his hearing deteriorated, he still used clear speech but also he learned how to use the deafblind manual alphabet to enable him to clarify any words that were unclear.

James

James was born profoundly Deaf. Until James had a car accident he communicated fluently using British Sign Language (BSL). The result of the accident was that he had acquired blindness. James felt isolated and became withdrawn because he could not use his usual method of communication. However, James learned how to use hands-on signing which empowered him.

Comment

These case studies highlight that while two people may have a similar 'sensory label', this need not indicate that their preferred method of communication will be similar. Both Richard and James experienced deafblindness; however Richard used clear speech and deafblind manual alphabet, while James used hands-on signing.

ACTIVITY 2.3

Look at the following case study for Grace. Again Grace has sight and hearing loss. Identify which communication method/s you feel would most likely be Grace's preferred method of communication. Critically reflect on why you made this choice. Would you change your choice after reflection?

CASE STUDY

Grace was born sighted and hearing. As she became older she became partially sighted and hard of hearing. Prior to experiencing sensory loss her primary form of communication was speech.

Comment

As people advance in age their sight and/or hearing can deteriorate (SENSE, 2007). Many of the people that you work with who are over 65 may experience a sight and/or hearing impairment. The way that each person deals with this situation will vary: some will adapt but others will find it difficult to cope with the sensory loss. Some people will admit there is a loss, others will not. However, whether we are working with a child or an adult, effective assessment is imperative. This will ensure that all aspects of an individual's sensory need are addressed and that intervention is 'person/need specific'. Other significant aspects of communication to address are the use of non-verbal, listening and observational communication methods (Trevithick, 2005).

As social workers, we need to have *everything at our disposal to come alongside the experiences of the people with whom we work* (Trevithick, 2005, p8). This is an interesting concept when analysing the requirements of people with sensory needs. For example, when communicating through sign language, non-verbal communication (sometimes referred to as body language) and facial expressions significantly enhance the way information is conveyed. Non-verbal communication should never be underestimated, as highlighted by Kadushin and Kadushin (1997), where they identify that *detailed studies have shown many items in non-verbal vocabulary including five thousand distinctly different hand gestures, and one thousand different steady body postures* (1997, p315).

ACTIVITY 2.4

Imagine you are at a lecture and the lecturer's voice is continually monotone. There is no modulation throughout the whole discourse. How interesting would you find that? Take time to visualise. Critically reflect on your thoughts and feelings. How could this situation have been improved?

Comment

The activity above highlights not only the importance of using modulation in our voices when communicating, but also the importance of using body language and facial gestures to modulate message conveyance in visual forms of communication such as sign language.

When using listening skills in communication it is important to note that there is a difference between hearing and listening. Hearing is the sense used to perceive sound, whereas listening is the act of hearing attentively. Lishman (1994) discusses active listening as meaning that the listener needs to be paying close attention to what is being communicated. However, Egan argues that *people want more than physical presence in human communication; they want the other person to be present psychologically, socially and emotionally* (Egan, 1990, p111). Trevithick (2005) explores the concept of 'non-selective' (sometimes referred to as non-directive or evenly suspended) listening. This type of listening is significant when working with sensory need as it refers to listening occurring at a number of different levels. This type of listening enables the listeners to be acute to what people are saying, how they say things, even what they are not saying. Trevithick describes this type of listening as *listening with the third ear ... and allows us to be sensitive to the wider social and cultural context from which an individual speaks* (Trevithick, 2005, p123).

Alisha was previously deaf with speech. Prior to becoming deafblind Alisha communicated using her voice, lipreading when communicating one-to-one and a British Sign Language (BSL) interpreter when attending meetings. Since becoming deafblind she now communicates using voice and a 'hands-on' signing interpreter. 'Hands-on' signing involves physical contact with the interpreter. The deafblind person places his/her hands over the hands of the signer to enable them to follow communication. Alisha's Asian culture does not allow physical contact with any male other than her husband.

ACTIVITY **2.5**

You are Alisha's social worker and she is attending a Disability Living Allowance (DLA) appeal and asks you to arrange for a 'hands-on' interpreter. Look at Trevithick's (2005) concept of 'the third ear'. What cultural needs would you take into account? How would you address this?

Comment

Observation is another important aspect of communication. Tanner and Le Riche (1998) highlight the value of observation in social work education and argue that observation could contribute to a more perceptive and critically conversant use of theoretical knowledge and procedures in practice. It could also be said to be a useful tool in hypothesis formulation about the things that we see or hear. Observation is not only used when observing others but can also be useful in self-observation (Sheldon, 1995). Self-observation can help us critically analyse our own practice and behaviours, and the impact our role has on the situation. We use observation all the time; sometimes it is conscious and sometimes unconscious. Conscious observation may be manifested when asking a colleague to carry out a joint visit to obtain a different perspective on a situation. Unconscious observations could take place as we arrive at the home of a person we will be working with in the form of environmental observations.

While all communicative methods impact on our practice, the key to good communication is to treat each person on an individual and equal basis. Koprowska (2005) discusses other temporary or permanent changes in communication, highlighting the need to take into account all communicative needs. For example, if a person has alphasia (inability to understand language, formulate and express thought), dementia (possible loss of memory for words, events and faces) or severe mental health problems, it is important to be aware that a variety of sensory differences can impact on communication (Koprowska, 2010). Conditions such as dysgeusia (the distortion or decrease of the sense of taste) and anosmia (the lack of or the inability to smell) can also impact on communication. An older person with dementia may be greatly disadvantaged if one or a number of sensory needs are absent as this may affect their ability to receive information. Next we will explore how vision and hearing can be maximised. We will be looking at using practical guidance and communication tips to capitalise on residual sight and sound.

Communication tips and practical guidance

Often sensory needs are hidden, for example unless a person who is blind or partially sighted wears glasses which indicate this, that person may appear sighted. If a deaf/Deaf person does not wear a hearing aid they may appear hearing. As highlighted earlier, every person uses a communication method that is individual to them. You may find the following tips helpful when communicating with any person who has a sensory need.

Broad-spectrum tips
- Attract the person's attention.
- Check preferred method of communication.
- Ensure there is no background noise. Switch off ambient noise, such as the television or radio.
- Be clear in your introduction.
- Rephrase/paraphrase.
- Be on time.
- Check you have been understood.
- Sit or stand at the same level at the person with the sensory need.
- Allow enough time to carry out the assessment – you may need more time when there is a sensory need.
- Use clear, straightforward speech.
- Avoid distractions – focus on the person you are communicating with.

If a person is Deaf/deaf/ hard of hearing or deafened

- Think of where you are seated. If you sit opposite a window, the light will shine on your face and make your lips easier to read. Make sure you are not sitting in shadow.

- Ensure hearing aid is on, that the batteries are working and the tubing is clean.

- Avoid shouting – use clear speech.

- Avoid bold patterns, dangly earrings, bright lipstick, graded lenses or sunglasses, especially if using sign language.

- Choose a quiet environment as extraneous noises may affect existing residual hearing.

- When talking, be face-to-face. Avoid having your head bent. Keep beards and moustaches trimmed. Avoid putting your hand over your mouth.

- If using sign language – remember it is unique to the individual. Some Deaf people may use signed supported English, others British Sign Language and others may mix the two or use an alternative/simplified version. Sign language is regional; avoid assuming every Deaf person will sign the same.

- Where possible try to produce information in DVD format using BSL.

- Children with a learning need may use Makaton or PECS (Pictorial Exchange Communication System). Often the school will have a 'communication passport' for the child outlining how to communicate effectively.

- Use play, painting or drawing.

If a person is blind or partially sighted

- Use clear speech.

- Does the person need to change their glasses? Is a magnifying glass needed?

- Consider producing information in Braille or audio.

- Use tactile forms of communication such as manual alphabet, block or hands-on signing.

If a person is deafblind

- If a person has Usher syndrome they may need time for their eyes to adjust to the light and time to focus into what they see.

- Hands-on signing, deafblind manual or block tactile communication.

- Objects of reference, e.g. a cup may indicate a person wants a drink.

Models and theoretical concepts

Davies highlights the importance of theory by arguing that social workers need to think theoretically to act clearly, competently and usefully in practical situations (Davies, 2002). However, sometimes models and theoretical concepts can seem daunting when a student is first acquiring a basis for practice, so to begin we will define what theory and models actually are.

Howe identifies a model as *a description or a phenomenon in which a low level of order is imposed to clarify information* (Howe, 1987). Howe also describes models as *bricks in theory building* (Howe, 1987, p10). Barker defines theory as *a group of related hypotheses, concepts, and constructs, based on facts and observations, that attempts to explain a particular phenomenon* (Barker, 2003, p34). Having identified what models and theoretical concepts are, we now explore the relationship between models, theories and communication in social work practice.

According to Fiske, *communication is too often taken for granted when it should be taken to pieces* (1994, pviii). As interaction is at the heart of social work, in this section we will explore and analyse models and theoretical concepts which broaden our understanding of communication within our work. Communication can come in many forms: body language (Lishman, 1994; Egan, 2002), phatic or small talk (Thompson, 2003), written (Derrida, 1976; Foucault, 1999), verbal (Trevithick, 2005) and many more. Within social work, concepts such as empathy, warmth and genuineness are vital to build a relationship which facilitates effective communication. These theoretical concepts are often linked with the works of Carl Rogers (1957) and Truax and Carkhuff (1967), who theorised that all intervention and involvement can have a profound impact, although we may never come to realise its full import. It could be argued this is the case when working with a person who experiences sensory need. Lack of empathy, warmth and genuineness can have a lasting impact on the person's perception of social work intervention.

CASE STUDY

Guy has a visual impairment. The social worker contacted Guy prior to his visit to discuss which format Guy would like the information he was bringing be presented in. Guy had asked the social worker to print the information on yellow paper and use font size 48 in bold black letters as this format maximised his use of vision. Guy was impressed that the social worker had taken time to contact him in advance to clarify the matter.

Comment

Guy's experience was a positive one. However, if the social worker had not addressed the issue of sensory need, the outcome could have been quite different. To explore this we will apply Shannon and Weaver's (1947) process approach to communication. The approach incorporates three aspects of communication: (1) the *transmitter* or the person initiating the communication; (2) the *receiver* or the person who receives the communication; and (3) the middle element referred to as 'noise'; 'noise' refers to any factors which influence the continuance or interference of communication (Thompson, 2003). It could be argued that this model is one of the simplest but most effective models used to explore communication, but it has been criticised for being simplistic and failing to address meaning (Thompson, 2003).

When a person has sight and hearing a literal noise can interfere with communication. For example when a person is in conversation with another and the telephone rings. The telephone is the 'noise' that interferes with the message being transmitted to the receiver. In Shannon and Weaver's model the point being conveyed is that a 'noise' is any factor that interferes with or prevents continuance of communication. These could include factors such as anger, anxiety, stress, sadness, power dynamics, class, gender, race, technical problems, information presented in formats not understood by the recipient or poor quality telephone lines (Thompson, 2003).

ACTIVITY **2.6**

Critically reflect on the case study of Guy. Reflect on Guy's sensory need and explore:

1. *Who is the transmitter?*

2. *Who is the receiver?*

3. *What could be the 'noise'?*

Comment

Communication is not merely about transmitting and receiving information; it is also about transmitting and receiving relationships. Pierre Bourdieu (1991) theorised on this when introducing the concept of 'habitus'. In this theory Bourdieu tries to explore understanding of the ways that people acquire sociological aspects to them as individuals, i.e. what they acquire through practice. He explored the importance of culture in relation to communication and talked of aspects of culture becoming like 'wallpaper'. The term 'wallpaper' referred to the capacity for the aspects of culture to blend into the background and while it is continually present it has little or no direct impact on the decisions we make either consciously or unconsciously. Bourdieu also talks about 'culture shock', which he describes as being in a cultural setting that makes one feel unsure of themselves. Bourdieu in his theory argues that the 'habitus' integrates a set of power relations outlining 'who speaks when', which is based on dominance and subordination and the impact these relations have on the whole persona. Bourdieu is theorising that it is not necessarily us that determine ideas, but rather that ideas are represented from the most dominant groups. He further explores the concepts that culture lives when meaningfully communicated, that there is a cultural capital which enables greater resources to draw on a culture and that there is the role of symbolic violence or the acceptance of domination. A significant aspect to Bourdieu's theory is that in communication all participants do not start on an equal footing. To illustrate, consider the following case study.

CASE STUDY

Eloise is a 22-year-old female. She is deafblind, has a mild learning disability and English is her second language. She has been referred by her local audiology department for an assessment by a care manager/social worker to see if there is any sensory equipment that could be of use to her. Eloise has enough residual sight and hearing to communicate verbally, but speech needs to be simple, clear, and concise with clear lip patterns. The social worker has booked an appointment for his visit but when he arrives he is accompanied by a male social work student and a male occupational therapist. Eloise did not realise there would be so many people and that they would all be male. To make matters worse, two of the men have beards which makes it difficult for her to read their lips. All three people are talking at the same time, using jargon, talking behind their hands and putting their heads down as they take things in and out of briefcases.

Critically reflect on Bourdieu's theory. What do you think the power dynamics are in this communicative situation? Do you think Eloise is experiencing positive, empowering communication?

Comment

An important aspect to remember with regard to theoretical concepts and models is not to become over-anxious as to what role they play in practice. Much of the time we use theories and models naturally without even thinking about it. Other times we may find we are being eclectic in our use of theory to enable us to provide unique and individual intervention. On other occasions we may find that critical reflection (Brown and Rutter, 2006) or reflecting in action (Schön, 1983) helps us to establish appropriate intervention. It is important to remember that as the social work role is complex by the very fact that we work with human beings, theoretical knowledge establishes a base line from which person-centred intervention can begin.

Cultural knowledge and clarification of how addressing cultural needs will lead to anti-discriminatory and anti-oppressive practice

As highlighted earlier in the case study of Alisha, culture has a significant place in communication. Guirdham defines culture as *a historically transmitted system of symbols, meanings and norms* (1999, p61). However, it could also be described as shared ideas, thoughts, communities, histories, traditions and language (BDA, 2007).

For most nationalities cultural recognition is significant. Even if a person either chooses or is forced by circumstances to move to a different country they often hold the culture they are born into or brought up in, close to their hearts.

Within a sensory setting, cultural recognition can be a significant factor. The importance of cultural recognition in communication may not be relevant in all sensory settings but it is apparent in some of them. To explain: someone who has acquired deafness possibly by presbyacusis (advancing years) or as a result of trauma will most likely not consider themselves to be part of a cultural sensory community. However, someone from the 'D' Deaf community may take a politicised stand on deafness and consider themselves to be part of a culturally Deaf community (Peters, 2000). The significance of culture in the Deaf community is explained by Paddy Ladd in *Disability politics* (Campbell and Oliver, 2006).

> *Basically Deaf people whose first language is BSL (British Sign Language) should be seen as a linguistic minority. It helps if you think of us as parallel to, say, an Asian community. Deaf people have been joyfully getting together since time began, and our schools go back to the 1970s and our clubs to the 1820s. Our language is much older. Deaf people marry each other 90 per cent of the time, and 10 per cent have Deaf children. Our customs and traditions have been passed down the ages and these, together with our values and beliefs, constitute our culture.*

(Campbell and Oliver, 2006, p120)

These words are echoed by Lois Bragg, a member of the Deaf community at Gallaudet University, in her address to a conference about disability culture. She argued that certain requirements needed to be met before a cultural identity could be achieved (Peters, 2000). These were:

- a common language;

- a historical lineage that can be traced textually (through archives, memorials and distinctive media/press publications);

- evidence of a cohesive social community;

- political solidarity;

- acculturation within the family at an early age (and/or in segregated residential schools and clubs);

- generational or genetic links;

- pride and identity in segregation from others.

Bragg argued that while these requirements did not exist in disability in general, they were present in the Deaf community. Thus she argued that while there is a Deaf culture there is not a disability culture. Peters (2000) critiqued this view and argues that *disability culture not only exists, but is a thriving concept and lived experience in the hearts and minds of many disabled people* (Peters, 2000, p584).

In the video, *Vital signs: crip culture talks back*, Carol Gill expressed her views on the concept that this is a disability culture. She says, *I believe very firmly in disabled culture and if we don't have one, we should. We need it to survive as an oppressed minority, both physically and emotionally* (Mitchell and Snyder, 1996).

Respect for diversity is essential for good practice regardless of whether cultural difference is sensory or otherwise. Understanding cultural perception and addressing these cultural needs is entirely individual and necessary to ensure anti-discriminatory and anti-oppressive practice.

D'Ardenne and Mahtani (1999) highlight the importance of *sensitivity to cultural variations, cultural knowledge of clients and reflecting the cultural needs of the client* (1999, p6). They further highlight that when a person has English as a second language, communication is disadvantaged. While some communities may not have the same opinion as this, others may concur that this is the case.

Owusu-Bempah and Howitt (2000) highlight that when addressing the needs of a black child in relation to cultural identity, psychosocial development and self-esteem, as social workers we should pay particular attention to the system or the environment in which a black child operates as a whole, rather than just focusing on their self-identity or self-esteem. This challenge is not always easy and Owusu-Bempah and Howitt (2000) describe it as complex and dynamic because we all have our own value bases. Whether the person we are working with is a child or an adult, all aspects of language and cultural diversity should be explored to ensure appropriate communication is facilitated.

In this section we have highlighted that in order to address the issue of communication in social work sensitively and appropriately, cultural knowledge and recognition of cultural beliefs are essential. It is important to recognise that we live in a multi-sensory, multi-cultural, multi-ethnic and multi-faith society and in order to deliver equality of service we need to ensure we have clear understandings of cultural issues. Heenan (2005) discusses social workers being *obliged to work within an anti-oppressive framework, addressing issues of oppression and discrimination* (2005, p495). Cultural knowledge and clarification of cultural need can therefore contribute to ensuring empathic, anti-discriminatory and anti-oppressive practice exists within social work.

Concepts of self-awareness and the impact these have on communicating in practice

Trevithick's (2005) concept of self-awareness allows thoughts, feelings and emotions associated with a case to be analysed and evaluated. Trevithick says that self-knowledge and self-awareness draw upon what we already know about ourselves, learning when we encounter new experiences and learning through our contact with others (Trevithick, 2005, p43). As professional values are influenced by anti-discriminatory and anti-oppressive practice (Parrott, 2007), an ethical issue would be to ensure practice intervention is empowering, appropriate and in partnership with the service user, their families/carers and other professionals. To ensure practice intervention is appropriate, self-awareness of communication methods used and how we respond to the communicative method used by others is imperative. A further concept of self-awareness is that of Cooley's (1902) *looking glass self.* Cooley explores how our actions and communications are mirrored back to us through others' responses. Trevithick and Cooley's concepts highlight the importance of ensuring appropriate communicative methods are used in practice, analysing service user/family/carer feedback, self-awareness, reflection and reflection in action (Schön, 1983).

Legislative frameworks and their impact on service delivery

Legislative framework impacts on service delivery when addressing communication needs in respect of a person with sensory requirements. An example of this in practice is in the Local Authorities and Social Services Act 1970 (Johns, 2005) which influenced guidance such as *Social care for deafblind children and adults* (DoH, 2001). Section 7 of the Act places responsibility on local authorities to: identify; make contact; keep records of deaf-blind people; offer appropriate services; provide one-to-one support (communicator guide); accessible formats (clear speech, bold print, British Sign Language, Braille); and overall responsibility by a senior manager (DOH, 2001). Bateman (2000) emphasises the importance of attaining effective assertiveness by getting the facts right and understanding appropriate policy and legislation. Specialist organisations such as the RNID, RNIB, SENSE or Deafblind UK ensure people are well informed about their rights and provide information to explore how to use legislation such as the Disability Discrimination Act 1995/2005 (Brayne and Carr, 2005) to promote change. An example of this is that all public information is now available in BSL format (RNID, 2007). Davies (2002) however, argues the Act is weak because it defines disability in terms of severity of impairment rather than experiences of discrimination. It could also be argued that the Human Rights Act 1998 is significant with regard to the law and communication as it is a human right of all adults and children with a sensory need to grow up as valued citizens and a significant contributory factor to this would be the provision of individual specialist communication.

Human aids to communication and technical equipment

In the course of our work we may find that we need specialist communicative intervention in order to carry out our intervention effectively and safely in the social work process. A variety of methods can be used.

Interpreters are used to translate from one language to another. Many Deaf people use British Sign Language (BDA, 2009), which as already explained is a language in its own right with its own grammatical structure, and use the interpreter to translate from one language to BSL and vice versa. The social worker needs to ensure an interpreter is present for the assessment/intervention and to book early to ensure interpreter availability. It is important to note when working with Deaf people that the term 'deaf and dumb' is obsolete and may be offensive to Deaf people; the term Deaf is more acceptable. It is not only Deaf people who use interpreters; it could be any individual with a sensory need. For example, a hard of hearing person may use a lipspeaker or a deafblind person may use a deafblind manual alphabet interpreter. The interpreter's role is to communicate everything that is being said and to 'voice over' in English everything the person with the sensory need communicates. Interpreters are usually trained professionals and work to a code of ethics, which includes impartiality, respect for diversity and confidentiality. An interpreter is not a social worker and will only communicate information spoken. The social worker should always speak 'directly' to the service user, addressing them in the first person, e.g. *It is nice to meet you*, rather than *Can you tell him/her it is nice to meet him/her?* It is important when using an interpreter in a group setting such as a Child in Need meeting or Adult Protection meeting for one person to speak at a time. This allows the interpreter to convey all information accurately, which is extremely important especially if the case goes to court.

Communicator guides work with people who have acquired dual sensory loss, i.e. deaf-blindness. Deafblind people often feel isolated and the communicator guides provide regular human contact, support and communication. The communicator guides are trained in deafblind awareness and in different communication methods, such as clear speech and deafblind manual alphabet (SENSE/Deafblind UK, 2009) and work to a code of ethics. The role of communicator guide is to enable the person with the dual sensory loss to communicate effectively with other people. A care manager/social worker may find that if they are working with an older service user who has acquired deafblindness, the person may feel more comfortable and at ease if their communicator guide is present. However, once again it is important to address the service user directly.

As a social worker we may encounter a *communication support worker* (CSW). They work in colleges, universities and some schools, helping deaf students to communicate with their teachers and other students. Their role is to support students by lipspeaking, note taking and interpreting between spoken English and British Sign Language (BSL); helping students understand and produce written material in class; adapting learning materials so that students understand them more easily; suggesting ways that the school or college environment can be improved to make it easier for students to use hearing aids or lipread, Council for the Advancement of Communication with Deaf People (CACDP). If a social worker is working with a child who has a CSW it may be useful to 'tap' into the expertise the CSW has to ensure that communication is effective.

The use of technical equipment such as a visual flashing or vibrating doorbell can be invaluable for a person with sensory need. Equipment can be a small intervention that can make a big difference. In the course of your work you may have encountered a visual doorbell system. This device enables a deaf/Deaf/blind or deafblind person to be alerted to the door by means of a visual door bell system (flashing light) or a vibrating pager system. This empowers the person with sensory need because it prevents the person being isolated and provides equality of opportunity for hearing/deaf/Deaf/visually impaired and deafblind people to be alerted to the door.

Technical equipment can also be fundamental in communication enhancement. For example:

- a loop;
- mini communicator;
- hearing aids (see Glossary for further details of technical equipment).

Remember to check if a person has any medical conditions before suggesting technical equipment. For example, a person with epilepsy may need to avoid strobe lighting devices and someone with a detached retina may need to avoid vibrating devices such as an under-pillow vibrating alarm clock. It is all about individuality and the need to assess/intervene on an individual basis. There may be an equipment officer for sensory need in your local authority, so it is good to explore this option for advice and information.

When communicating with whichever is the chosen method, be sensitive; show respect and where possible talk directly to the service user. Don't be afraid to ask questions; really listen; you may feel embarrassed but stay calm. Watzlawick et al. (1974) argue that mistakes in communication are widespread and that context is often missed. However, remember it takes two or more to communicate and it is better to attempt communication than not try at all. Give equal value to signing, eye contact, facial expression and touch. Ineffective communication can have disastrous consequences (Laming, 2003), while effective communication can have positive results (BDA/SENSE/Deafblind UK/RNIB, 2007). It is essential that all workers take time to address this issue and remember that communication is a two-way street.

Koprowska, J (2010) *Communication and interpersonal skills in social work.* Third edition. Exeter: Learning Matters.

This book is part of the Transforming Social Work Practice series written specifically to support students on social work degree courses. The honours degree in social work requires all students to learn communication skills with children, adults and those with communication difficulties, and have these skills assessed. This book is an interactive source and is very practical in approach, with activities and case studies throughout the text. The case study summaries of contemporary research and theory illustrate and draw out key points, to aid and reinforce learning.

Trevithick, P (2005) *Social work skills: A practice handbook.* Second edition. Maidenhead: Open University Press/McGraw-Hill Education.

This book has been written by an experienced academic-practitioner. It provides descriptions of over 50 social work skills, with case examples to illustrate their creative use in practice. This edition contains material on social work methods, practice approaches and perspectives, the knowledge base of social work and the importance of the relationship between theory and practice. The starting point for this text is that social work is – and has to be – a highly skilled activity. It is important to stress this fact because social work practitioners work with some of the most complex, unpredictable and troubling areas of human experience. For this reason social work is also an intellectual activity. This book provides practitioners with the 'toolbox' of skills to assist them with becoming effective practitioners.

Thompson, N (2003) *Communication and language. A handbook of theory and practice.* Basingstoke: Palgrave Macmillan.

Communication and language are fundamental aspects of working life, especially for those working with people and their problems in a variety of settings. In this book, Neil Thompson explores the complexities of the considerable theory base underpinning communication and language, demonstrating how theoretical ideas can be applied in practice. In 'people work', success often depends on how effectively we are able to communicate, while serious problems can be seen to arise when communication breaks down. Developing our knowledge and skills in relation to communication and language is therefore an important goal to pursue. With its strong practice focus, and its emphasis on reflection and its suggestions for further reading, this book can play an important part in that pursuit. A truly interesting and innovative book.

Healy, K (2005) *Social work theories in context: Creating frameworks for practice.* Basingstoke: Palgrave Macmillan.

This book provides an integrated and flexible framework for practice which links theory, context and skills. Guiding the reader through a wide range of social work theory, it emphasises the application of theory to practice throughout. It assesses the key discourses and contemporary theories that inform current practice, considering approaches such as problem-solving, the strengths perspective, radical and anti-oppressive practice and postmodernism. Presenting social work as a diverse activity that is profoundly shaped by public policies, service missions and practice locations, this book offers an original, up-to-date analysis that will enlighten current and future social work practice.

Chapter 3

Discrimination faced by people with sensory needs

Introduction

This chapter explores discrimination experienced by people with sensory needs, within a theoretical and historical context. It is essential that a thorough understanding of this is achieved, as social work practitioners operate within complex human situations (Parker and

Bradley, 2005). The International Association of the School of Social Work (IASSW) and the International Federation of Social Workers (IFSW) 2001 define the social work role in the following way.

> *The social work profession promotes social change, problem-solving in human relationships and the empowerment and liberation of people to enhance well-being. Utilising theories of human behaviour and social systems, the social worker intervenes at the points where people interact with their environments. Principles of human rights and social justice are fundamental for social work.*

> (Parker and Bradley, 2005, p3)

We will begin by examining how people with sensory needs have been viewed at different points in history and asking you to consider how these stereotypes may still continue in modern society.

The discrimination currently faced by people with sensory needs will be explored and the role of legislation will be examined. Case studies will be used to illustrate the impact of discrimination and to help you consider how this can be challenged through promotion of anti-discriminatory practice.

Medical and social models of disability will be examined in depth to provide you with different ways of understanding disability. As the medical model focuses on *physical deficits and individual health needs the challenge for social work practitioners is not to fall into 'disablest perceptions' by accepting this model* (Parker and Bradley, 2005, p76). The move towards a social model of disability in many areas of service provision has been crucial to developments in disability services in recent years and you will be asked to consider the extent to which this is true in services for people with sensory needs.

This chapter will focus on sensory needs in terms of blindness, deafness and deafblindness (please see Glossary and Chapter 1 for definitions). It is important to note that there is a proper distinction between the term *Deaf* with a capital '*D*' and *deaf* with a lower case '*d*'.

A person who considers themselves to be Deaf would most likely be a profoundly deaf person who would not consider themselves to be disabled, but rather part of a minority group with their own culture, history and linguistics (British Deaf Association, 2007). This was highlighted by the British Deaf Association (BDA) when British Sign Language (BSL) attained official language status on 18 March 2003. Deaf people see being Deaf as part of their heritage and most likely consider themselves proud to be deaf.

A deaf person is likely to have been a previously hearing person or one who was born deaf, growing up in a hearing family with oral communication being the primary means of communication. A person who has previously experienced the ability to hear music, voices and birds singing and then becomes profoundly deaf, for example as a result of meningococcal infection, would likely be traumatised. The individual may experience loss and bereavement (Kübler-Ross, 1976) and feel they have suffered a personal tragedy and therefore label themselves as disabled.

Historical context of discrimination and stigma experienced by people with sensory needs

We shall be exploring the historical context of discrimination and stigma experienced by people with sensory needs. Knowledge of this is vital because, as Parker and Bradley remind us, *risk assessment and risk management are an integral aspect of the social work process* (Parker and Bradley, 2005). Understanding discrimination and stigma in terms of individual need can affect the assessment process and in turn have a significant impact on the individual themselves. Initially, we need to examine what we mean by the terms discrimination and stigma.

Discrimination

Legislation is important because it states *what the government expects and requires of local authorities in relation to good practice* (Trevithick, 2005, p17). The Disability Discrimination Act 1995/2005 defines discrimination as treating an individual less favourably than treating another. In the case of a person with a disability, a person is being discriminatory if they fail to comply with a duty to make a reasonable adjustment in relation to the disabled person. However, in moral and political philosophy, the expression 'discrimination' is often restricted to the unfavourable treatment of particular groups of individuals, on prejudiced and irrelevant grounds.

Stigma

Stigma has been defined as a *deeply discrediting trait which may also be called a failing, a shortcoming, or a handicap* (Higgins, 1980, p123). The term 'stigma' originally referred to physical marks that were cut or burned into the skins of criminals, slaves and traitors to visibly identify them as different. Within social work, we use the term to refer to the ways in which individuals and groups can be labelled as different.

Discriminatory attitudes towards people with sensory needs have a long history. Under ancient Roman law, deaf people were classified as *mentecatti furiosi* (literally, 'raving maniacs') and were claimed to be 'uneducable' (Gracer, 2003).

Milestones

Fourth century AD	The first known tactile alphabet for blind people was made by 'Didymus the blind', an Egyptian scholar who carved letters out of wood.
Seventh century AD	The Venerable Bede wrote an account of the earliest known attempt to teach a deaf child in Europe by his contemporary St John of Beverly.
1550	The world's first school for deaf people was established by the Benedictine monk, Pedro Ponce de Leon, at the monastery of San Salvador, near Madrid, Spain.
1760	Thomas Braidwood established the first academy for deaf people in Edinburgh, which was renowned for teaching 'oralism' (speech) and written skills to students. While the introduction of this oral way of teaching benefited some deaf/Deaf people, it was to impact on attitudes that exist in contemporary society and impede the natural use of sign language for other deaf/Deaf people.

1784	Valentin Hauy opened the first school for blind people in Paris, introducing modern formal education to blind people.
1817	Thomas Hopkins Galludet and Laurent Clerc co-founded the first American school for the Deaf in Hartford, Connecticut.
1837	Laura Bridgeman (who became the first known deafblind person to be successfully educated), enrolled at the Massachusetts Institute for the Blind.
1856	Gallaudet University was established by Amos Kendall in 1856 (re-named Galludet University in 1986). This bilingual community – in which both American sign language and English coexist – was the first school for the advanced education of the deaf and hard-of-hearing in the world. It is still the world's only university in which all programmes and services are specifically designed to accommodate deaf and hard-of-hearing students (Galludet University, 2008).
1981	The United Kingdom's Disabled People's Council is the UK's national organisation of the worldwide Disabled People's Movement. Organised by disabled people to promote full equality and participation in UK society.
1995	Disability Discrimination Act (DDA)1995 is passed. (This will be explored further, later in the chapter.)
1999	Community Care (Direct Payments) Act 1996 is passed which enabled local authorities to make direct payments (cash payments) to individuals to enable them to secure provision of care in lieu of social services provision. Disability Rights Commission Act is passed.
2001	Special Educational Needs and Disability Act is passed, promoting the education of children with disabilities in mainstream schools (Swain et al., 2007).
2003	BSL is recognised as an official British language.
2005	Amendment of DDA extended the Act to include employment, education and access to goods, facilities and services. (This will be explored further, later in the chapter.)
2007	Equality and Human Rights Commission is now responsible for helping secure civil rights for disabled people since the closure of the Disability Rights Commission on 28 September 2007.

ACTIVITY **3.1**

What themes can you locate within the historical developments outlined above? Do you find the same issues reoccurring throughout history?

Comment

One theme is about specialist vs mainstream services. Looking at the field of education, the first developments were regarding provision of specialist education to people with sensory needs. This provision was segregated from mainstream educational services, although it was not until 1872 in the UK that free, compulsory mainstream education became accessible on a universal scale for children aged 5–13 years.

A similar theme is the tension between encouraging children with hearing impairments to develop speech, and the development of British Sign Language (BSL) and other alternative forms of communication. The first academy for deaf students (developed in Edinburgh in 1760), promoted children being taught speech, but this caused controversy because it discouraged the use of any form of sign language. This tension between separatist and integrationist responses is clearly seen in the debate around deaf/Deaf. People who define themselves as 'Deaf' argue that they are a separate community with their own recognised language, BSL.

A third theme is the growing recognition of discrimination faced by people with sensory needs and the need to challenge it through legislation and awareness raising. This reflects the increasing role of the state to legislate and intervene to protect the rights of disabled people.

A fourth theme is the development of the disability movement and user-run organisations.

Explore how people with sensory needs face discrimination

As you read through the historical context, it is easy to imagine that the situation for people with sensory needs has improved considerably. While there is some truth in this, it is important to recognise that significant levels of discrimination still exist. Some is overt and intentional, but much is due to lack of awareness and poor policies and practice. This is reflected by Postle (2002), who questions *how far care management practice is currently meeting older people's needs* (Postle, 2002, p348). Therefore it could be argued that discrimination could arise from lack of awareness, which in turn leads to ineffective practice. It could also be argued that services are not sensory-aware because of the environmental barriers imposed upon them due to the care management system of *working under strain* (Carey, 2003, p121).

CASE STUDY

Alice is 98 years old, is deafblind and is living in a nursing home. While people experience different levels of sight and hearing loss, Alice has become profoundly deaf and severely sight impaired (able to see bold outlines, e.g. very large dark font): this is called acquired deafblindness. This level of sensory disablement indicates that Alice is unable to read books, watch TV or communicate with people who are not deafblind aware. This means that Alice does not choose her own food or socialise. Additionally, Alice now has mobility difficulties which means she is unable to mobilise independently. The staff at the nursing home are not deafblind aware and therefore suppose that Alice is isolating herself by choice. Prior to becoming deafblind and immobile, Alice had a good job, enjoyed socialising and had an adventurous nature, visiting a variety of far-away destinations. Now she is in a nursing home, lonely and isolated.

ACTIVITY 3.2

You are a specialist assessor who has come to the nursing home to assess Alice. How might you approach assessing and meeting Alice's sensory needs and how would you address these with the staff team?

Comment

Social work is a practical role which focuses on protecting people and altering their lives (Parker and Bradley, 2005). Within sensory need theoretical application is essential to address and overcome environmental barriers that arise from sensory need (Bronfenbrenner, 1979, in Crawford and Walker, 2004). Therefore, it could be argued that if the environment barrier is addressed, then the sensory need can be met. To illustrate, let's look at Alice's case. An individual, specialist sensory assessment revealed the nursing home where Alice resided, was 'not' deafblind aware. Thus a programme was put together, which included the following measures:

- Sensory awareness training for staff members.

- An agreement was made to use a personalised communication scheme for Alice by using bold print (e.g. very large, dark font) communication cards (pictures of bed, meals, drinks, etc.) and an individual training programme for the manager and staff. The staff agreed that prior to addressing Alice's needs they would alert her of their presence by touching her hand. Next, show her the card of the task they were performing (e.g. 'meal'), then carry out the task.

- The activities worker at the nursing home became involved when she ordered dominoes for blind people (raised numbers) and agreed to play on a one-to-one basis, which was supported by the registered manager.

- To avoid isolation, a regular volunteer visit was arranged to provide Alice with an opportunity to talk about any subject she chose. While her level of sensory loss was profound, she had many memories of her previous adventures and travels. When a person has sight, facial gestures play an important role in receiving information. When a person does not have this sense, an alternative communication method is required. Tactile communication, such as a touch to the hand, enabled Alice to be aware that the volunteer was present and varying degrees of pressure to the hand indicated that attention was being paid to what Alice was saying. Living with acquired profound disability impacted on Alice as it prevented her from reading, listening to the radio, watching television, or conversing with the other residents/staff.

- All of these measures were regularly monitored and reviewed.

While much of the literature about the integration of people with disabilities focuses upon older people, the area of parenthood is important but receives less attention.

RESEARCH SUMMARY

Parents with a visual impairment

Gutman (2007) argues that much of the literature about parents with a disability has been grounded in a medical model of disability, emphasising the perceived incompetence and difficulties experienced by disabled parents. In this study, 70 parents with visual impairment were interviewed and the following themes were identified.

- ***Experiences with transportation*** *Two-thirds of parents identified challenges around using transport. Parents reported negative responses by bus and taxi drivers and other*

continued

passengers. One father reported problems during the winter months because bus drivers would often stop next to puddles and not realising, he and his children often got wet feet.

- **Experience of other people's attitudes** *Half of the parents reported discriminatory attitudes in relation to their parenting role. Many expressed feeling hurt by negative comments by sighted people that implied that they were 'helpless, needy or cognitively impaired'. They described intrusive questioning that would not be experienced by sighted parents, e.g. being asked how they bathed or dressed their children. Often other people would undermine their status as parents by disciplining their children while they were present or tying their shoelaces without asking permission. Parents described interactions with health care staff around the birth, in which staff spoke only to their sighted attendants. After the birth, they reported being questioned intensively about their ability to look after their child and feeling that they had to prove their abilities more than a sighted person. One parent stated* Everything is pressure ... if there's a stain on the child's clothing ... maybe it's neglect ... I have to prove I can function perfectly.

- **Psychosocial issues** *More than a third of parents talked about their children being teased at school or labelled as* those kids with the blind parents. *One father described how his daughter would discourage him from attending parents' meetings because she thought others would laugh at him.*

- **Health and safety issues** *More than a quarter spoke of their anxieties regarding the health and safety of their children, e.g. giving their child medication, monitoring physical systems and navigating the medical system when their child is ill.*

- **Positive aspects of being a parent with visual impairment** *Nearly two-thirds of parents identified positive aspects of being a parent with visual impairment. For example, a child learning that they need to talk to communicate and many parents being proud of their child's increased verbal skills. Some parents identified their children as demonstrating increased acceptance of difference and discussed being positive role models for their children by demonstrating on a daily basis that they are able to manage despite the difficulties. Some parents were able to discuss their sense of accomplishment in being able to succeed in the parenting role and their sense of pride in enjoying the successes of their children.*

It could be argued that if social care needs of visually impaired parents are left unmet, social exclusion and discriminatory attitudes could be exacerbated, thus preventing equality of opportunity (Percival and Hanson, 2005).

Organisations such as the RNIB are proactive in their aims for challenging blindness and empowering people who are blind or partially sighted. They actively campaign to remove barriers that blind and partially sighted people face in an effort to challenge discrimination and promote equality.

The Department of Health updated the mechanism for registering people as blind or partially sighted in response to active campaigning. The result was that the following clarifications were introduced:

- Certificate of Vision Impairment (CVI) form is signed by a consultant ophthalmologist in order to register someone as sight impaired/partially sighted or as severely sight impaired/blind. This provides the formal notification required by councils with social services responsibilities or their agents.

- The Department also introduced two documents: the Low Vision Leaflet (LVL) and the Referral for Visual Impairment (RVI) to facilitate easier access to support services prior to certification.

(DoH, 2005)

Thus, it appears that social care issues that are raised and challenged by specialist organisations such as the RNIB are essential to promoting equality and challenging discrimination.

As initially discussed, much of the literature about disability has been grounded in a medical model of disability. It is therefore crucial when addressing social care needs to critically analyse the dominant models of disability, these being the social and the medical models of disability.

Examination of medical and social models of disability in the context of anti-discriminatory practice

Why do we need to examine models of disability in the context of anti-discriminatory practice? People with disabilities are recognised as a minority group, collectively experiencing discrimination and oppression, rather than individuals who have experienced a personal tragedy. The model of disability that we adopt will influence our practice and thus impact on our concept of discrimination and oppression and affect our ability to facilitate change (Brown and Rutter, 2006).

Macdonald (1972) defines disability as the *condition of being unable to perform, as a consequence of, physical or mental unfitness*. The Union of the Physically Impaired Against Segregation (UPIAS) (1976) argues that disability is:

The disadvantage or restriction of activity caused by a contemporary social organisation which takes no or little account of people who have a physical impairment and thus excludes them from participation in the mainstream of social activities. Physical disability is therefore a particular form of social oppression.

(p14)

Analysing these definitions reveals that Macdonald's definition views disability from a medical model, assuming that difficulties faced by the disabled person are as a direct result of their individual impairment (Davies, 2002). The UPIAS definition embraces the social model of disability, which switches focus away from any physical limitations the impairment presents and onto physical and social environmental limitations, thus promoting the person and the political empowerment of disabled people (Oliver and Sapey, 2006). Regrettably, the medical model is dominant (Davies, 2002), thus living with disability becomes a constant struggle.

Models of disability give us a structure for critically reflecting (Brown and Rutter, 2006) on the way in which people with physical, psychological and sensory needs experience disability. Additionally, your own attitudes and values will affect your social work practice in relation to how you personally apply theoretical models of disability (Crawford and Walker, 2004). Exploring and understanding these models also enables individual and societal frameworks for legislation, processes and structures to be developed to facilitate change to the lives of disabled people (French and Swain, 2008; Oliver and Sapey, 2006). As discussed earlier, the models we will be considering are the medical and social models of disability.

A medical model approach to disability is inclined to centre on either the biological or psychological aspects of disability (Bernstein, 2007; Brabyn et al., 2007). The social model of disability is inclined to focus on cultural or structural aspects of disability (Priestley, 2003).

ACTIVITY 3.3

Look at the following definitions of disability. Which model of disability do they correspond to?

1. Disability *is the condition of being unable to perform as a consequence of physical or mental unfitness (Macdonald, 1972).*

2. Disability *is the disadvantage or restriction of activity caused by a contemporary social organisation which takes no or little account of people who have a physical impairment and thus excludes them from participation in the mainstream of social activities. Physical disability is therefore a particular form of social oppression (The Union of the Physically Impaired Against Segregation, 1976, p14).*

Comment

Although the two definitions were produced at a similar time, they represent radically different views about the nature of disability. The first definition corresponds to the medical model, focusing on what individuals are unable to do. The second definition corresponds to the social model and focuses on the disabling barriers that exclude disabled people from mainstream activities (Oliver and Sapey, 2006). Davies (2002) argues that the medical model remains dominant, though the social model has received increased support through legislation such as the Disability Discrimination Act 1995/2005.

In social care the predominant model of disability used is the social model of disability. This is primarily because the social care profession recognises that disability is not a case of mending something that has broken but rather overcoming societal barriers to enable a person with a disability to be treated as favourably as others to whom that disability does not or would not apply (DDA 1995/2005). To underpin practice from a social model perspective (Davies, 2002), social environmental barriers need to be removed.

> ### CASE STUDY
>
> *William was finding it difficult to read the newspaper. He had never experienced a problem before so he decided to visit the optician and get his eyes tested. The optician advised him that it was normal for him to experience a slight deterioration in his eyesight as he was get-ting older, and provided him with a prescription for reading glasses. While William did not particularly want to wear glasses he knew that many of his associates, friends and family also had reading glasses. He went to the glasses frames showroom to look at an array of frames and chose one. William thought his choice of frame made him look very distinguished.*

Comment

William's barrier was his deterioration in eyesight. The barrier was removed when he wore the prescriptive glasses. As so many people have this experience, spectacles or glasses are considered an acceptable intervention by the majority of people. However, this is still removal of a social environmental barrier because when William goes to a restaurant he can put on his glasses and make his own choices: he is autonomous.

Oliver (1996) indicates that *disability according to the social model is all the things that impose restrictions on a disabled person* (1996, p33). This could be on a personal level or a societal one. It could be in the form of inaccessibility to buildings, unusable transport facili-ties or information provided in an inappropriate format for a person with sensory needs.

The medical model of disability places emphasis on the physical condition being intrinsic to the individual. Critically reflect (Brown and Rutter, 2005) on the medical profession's primary role which is to cure, manage, identify, and understand a person's physical condi-tion in order to control or modify its course. In this quest the health care service invests much time and money in an attempt to cure illness and disability in a bid to enhance an individual's life and enable them to experience as normal a life as possible. Disability is seen in terms of impairment and loss (Lessoni et al., 2005).

Lessoni et al. (2005) conducted a study exploring the responses of US medical students about their attitudes to disability. The research was carried out using focus groups and interviews (Robson, 2007). The sample size was limited due to geographical constraints and thus the results might have been different with a larger sample size. The study found that the majority of students mentioned disabilities in an empathic and caring context. However, the students also contributed negative views of living with disability, such as perceiving loss, frustration, isolation and depression as possible outcomes of disability. Further, they did not fully understand that environmental barriers could exacerbate the disability.

However, while it may appear that the medical model focuses on disability as something needing to be fixed, Williams (2007) highlights that the medical model is also central to research into prevention of certain conditions.

> **CASE STUDY**
>
> *Chloe was born hearing. When she was 18 months old she contracted measles and lost 85 per cent of her hearing. Chloe is now 3 years old and about to attend nursery school. The ear, nose and throat consultant suggested cochlear implants. Chloe and her family underwent a series of psychological and physical assessments and it was agreed that Chloe would receive implants. Chloe with the implants now receives a level of sound to enable her to progress at nursery.*

Comment

The consultant was working from a medical model of disability, defining the hearing loss as an abnormality (Williams, 2007) which needed to be cured. The fact that the medical profession viewed this hearing condition as an impairment meant that a way to 'fix' the problem was explored. Therefore the impact of acoustic nerve stimulation was investigated. Much work was dedicated to this field as it was originally discovered by French-Algerian surgeons Andre Djourno and Charles Eyries in the 1950s, improved by an American doctor, William F House, during the 1960s and developed by a Melbourne University researcher, Graeme Clarke, in the 1970s. The result of this intervention is that today a significant number of people who are profoundly deaf or severely hard of hearing are provided with a degree of sound because the medical profession worked from the medical model and viewed hearing loss as an impairment, a disability that needed to be rectified.

Lessoni et al. (2005) discussed that while people in general try to avoid blatant forms of discrimination insidious discrimination still takes place.

> **CASE STUDY**
>
> *Alistair was a care home worker on minimum wage and travelled to work using local transport. He enjoyed his work and felt that he treated all the service users equally and fairly – in an anti-discriminatory way.*
>
> *One of the residents, Sid, was visually impaired and could no longer read the small print on his newspaper. Alistair ensured that Sid received the newspaper regularly on audio tape so that he remained informed and could contribute to group discussions about world events. One day it was announced that the local transport fares were going to be increased by 30 per cent to enable funding to be allocated to provide access for disabled people in the local shopping centre. While Alistair worked and generally treated disabled people in an anti-discriminatory way, critically reflect how he would feel if this way of practising directly affected him personally.*

PCS model

Sensory disability is often an invisible disability (SENSE, 2007). If a person can see a disability such as a person in a wheelchair or with Down syndrome (Thomson et al., 1995; Anderson, 2001), it is easier for them to comprehend the difficulties experienced by an individual. Thompson (2006) highlights the tendency to ignore the wider cultural and structural factors surrounding a person with a disability and also the dangers of pathologising; seeing the problem as being with the person themselves.

CASE STUDY

Roger is deafblind and has had bad experiences with people with pushchairs. The person pushing the pushchair gets impatient when he does not move out of their way (reason being he has not seen them or heard them). His experience has been that people get exasperated and push past him. Roger has no visible physical disabilities but he is deafblind and has mobility difficulties. The person pushing past him unbalances him, not even realising the impact that she/he is having on Roger.

Thompson's (2006) PCS model helps in practice to understand the level of discrimination Roger is experiencing.

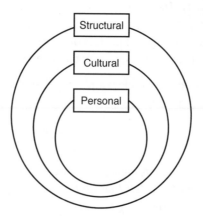

Figure 3.1 PCS model

Source: Thompson, 2006, p22

Thompson draws our attention to the fact that understanding internalisation helps practitioners to make sense of the reality external factors place on disabled people (Thompson, 2006). As indicated by Figure 3.1, Thompson analyses how structural, cultural and personal factors influence attitudes and perceptions. If these factors are not taken into account the disabled person can experience discrimination and oppression. Take the example of Roger (discussed above), as he is being affected on personal, cultural and structural levels.

CASE STUDY

Roger had a successful career and social life which has become more restricted. In addition, he feels that society does not understand the implications of deafblindness and therefore does not make allowances for it. The illustration of the person with the pushchair highlights Roger's plight. Critically applying this model into practice with Roger highlighted that he was experiencing discrimination because he was not being seen on a personal level in the perspective of an individual person (Crawford and Walker, 2007), which is a man who is deafblind with mobility difficulties. The cultural discrimination emerged because as a relatively young man Roger was expected to behave in an able-bodied manner and this did not take into account his disabilities. Finally on a structural level, Roger was experiencing inequalities in relation to power and influence because he felt disempowered in an able-bodied environment.

Thompson's exploration of the PCS model highlights that individual behaviour needs to be understood not just by social work practitioners, but every area of society encompassing a wider cultural and social context because these impact on an individual at a personal level (Thompson, 2006).

Disability Discrimination Act 1995/2005

The socio-political environment has influenced discrimination faced by people with sensory needs (Priestley, 2003). In the UK legislation has fulfilled an important function in attempting to fight discrimination and empower disabled people at both societal and individual levels. However, does conforming to normalisation undermine respect for diversity and reflexive consumerism (Priestley, 2003)? Or is this conformation needed in order to access equality? It could be argued that reflexive consumerism presents opportunities for consumers/service users to be more autonomous with how they see themselves and how they identify their personal need. This in turn will impact on the social work process of assessment, planning, intervention and review (Parker and Bradley, 2005) and ultimately impinge on the service that the individual receives.

There are five main legislative acts that service providers and employers must consider to avoid discriminating against disabled people. This also includes people with sensory needs. These are:

- *Equality Act 2006* (Gov.UK 2006);

- *Disability Discrimination Act* (DDA) *1995* and *2005 Amendment*;

- *Care Standards Act 2002;*

- *Building Regulations Act 1992;*

- *British Standard B8300 2002*
(Johns, 2005; Brayne and Carr 2005)

For the purpose of this section we will be focusing on the DDA 1995/2005. However, we will briefly address the other pieces of legislation as they impact on discrimination that may arise for the people we work with.

Social care workers should be aware that the Care Standards Act 2002 places a duty on care homes to provide adaptations and equipment for residents, including aids to communication, such as an induction loop system. Additionally, current building regulations stipulate that newly built or substantially reconstructed, non-domestic buildings must also provide aids for people with sensory disabilities. Once again this could be in the form of a loop system. The new code of practice BS8300 (2002) which links into the Building Regulations Act 1992 again instructs that the needs of disabled people are to be met, including people with sensory needs. The Equality Act 2006 promotes understanding of equality and diversity and enforces the quality enactments and works toward the elimination of unlawful discrimination.

Under the terms of the DDA (1995/2005) reasonable adjustments must be made to provide full access to goods or services for people with sensory needs. The 2005 amendment builds on the existing civil rights legislation of the 1995 Act. From October 2004 it became a legal requirement to permanently install induction loops and other forms of equipment in public areas and in the workplace.

The Act also enforces that employers must ensure that existing and potential employees are not at a disadvantage in the workplace. Since 1 October 2004 all employers have a duty to ensure that disabled people are not treated less favourably than others for any reason relating to their disability, unless this can be warranted. An example of this is taking part in meetings.

CASE STUDY

Emma is severely hard of hearing. She wears two hearing aids, one in her left ear and one in her right ear. Emma has recently been invited to attend a seminar.

While the seminar is organised by her current employer, the venue is not one Emma has attended previously. Emma can communicate effectively on a one-to-one basis but when it comes to large groups she finds her hearing aids amplify all sounds. This presents difficulties for Emma because the environmental/background noises and speech intermingle and distort the sound. Prior to the seminar the organiser sent Emma a pre-attendance request for any additional requirements. Emma requested access to a loop system. The loop system is a device which enables people with a hearing loss to obtain maximum involvement in communication in the environment in which the loop is fitted. The loop has a microphone, an amplifier and loop wire which is installed around the area being served. The receiver would usually be Emma's hearing aid. The hearing aid would be set to the 'T' position or cinema position as children tend to call it.

ACTIVITY 3.4

Look at the case study of Emma. What was Emma's sensory need? What action was taken to ensure that Emma was not discriminated against in the workplace? What legislation was used to support this action?

Comment

The issue of discrimination is a very serious one, and if it is not adhered to, the Equality and Human Rights Commission itself may choose to take legal action in extreme cases of discrimination. As social work practitioners, challenging oppression and discrimination should be integral to our practice as we strive to promote social change, solve problems and empower people to augment their welfare (Parker and Bradley, 2005).

C H A P T E R   S U M M A R Y

This chapter has explored how people with sensory needs face discrimination., It has provided an historical context to enlighten and explain why particular attitudes exist today and examined medical and social models of disability in the context of anti-discriminatory practice. Additionally, it has highlighted how use of the PCS model (Thomson, 2001) can promote understanding of how discrimination affects an individual on personal, cultural and structural levels, and how use of legislation can promote anti-discriminatory social work practice.

Case studies were used to demonstrate integration to practice and assist the reader to visualise discrimination that is faced by people with a sensory need. The chapter has highlighted not only that sensory awareness is essential for workers, regardless of which discipline they come from, but also the need to challenge discrimination and practice in an anti-discriminatory way.

FURTHER READING

French, S and Swain, J (2007) *Understanding disability: A guide for health professionals*. London: Elsevier Health Sciences.

This book, which relates to health care policy and practice, is based on the social rather than the medical model of disability. The book further views disability in terms of environmental, structural and attitudinal barriers which deny disabled people full participation in society. Case studies and activities throughout facilitate understanding of issues presented.

Swain, J, Barnes, C, French, S and Thomas, C (2004) *Disabling barriers, enabling environments*. Second edition. London: Sage.

This book has been revised to provide an up-to-date and accessible introductory text to the field of disability studies. In addition to analysing the barriers that disabled people encounter in education, housing, leisure and employment, the revised edition has chapters on international issues, diversity among disabled people, sexuality and bioethics.

Parker, J and Bradley, G (2010) *Social work practice: Assessment, planning, intervention and review*. Third edition. Exeter: Learning Matters.

This accessible book enables social work students to gain knowledge of assessment, planning, intervention and review, to reflect on that knowledge and apply it in practice. It is an interactive book that encourages the reader to reflect on learning needs and to consider the development of career-long professional learning and use case studies as a means to examine theories and models for social work practice.

Brown, K and Rutter, L (2006) *Critical thinking for social work*. Exeter: Learning Matters.

Critical thinking as a process can appear formal, academic, and far removed from everyday life where decisions have to be taken quickly in less than ideal conditions. Critical thinking is, however, a vital part of social work. This book takes a pragmatic look at a range of ideas associated with critical thinking. The text is innovative, interesting and thought-provoking and can aid students to embrace the concept of critical thinking.

Chapter 4

Sensory awareness in adult services

ACHIEVING A SOCIAL WORK DEGREE

This chapter will help to meet the following National Occupational Standards.

Key Role 2: Plan, carry out, review and evaluate social work practice, with individuals, families, carers, groups, communities and other professionals.

- Interact with families, carers, groups and communities to achieve change and development and to improve life opportunities.
- Work with groups to promote individual growth, development and independence.

Key Role 6: Demonstrate professional competence in social work practice.

- Work within the principles and values underpinning social work practice.
- Identify and assess issues, dilemmas and conflicts that might affect your practice.
- Devise strategies to deal with ethical issues, dilemmas and conflicts.

This chapter will also assist you to follow the GSCC (General Social Care Council) Codes of Practice for Social Care Workers.

GSCC Code 1: As a social care worker you must protect the rights and promote the interests of service users and carers.

- Treating each person as an individual.
- Respecting and, where appropriate, promoting the individual views and wishes of both service users and carers.
- Supporting service users' rights to control lives and make informed choices about the services they receive.
- Respecting and maintaining the dignity of the service users and carers.
- Respecting diversity and different culture and values.

GSCC Code 6: As a social care worker you must be accountable for the quality of your work and take responsibility for maintaining and improving your knowledge and skills.

- Meeting relevant standards of practice and working in a lawful, safe and effective way.
- Maintaining clear and accurate records as required by procedures established for your work.
- Recognising and respecting the roles and expertise of workers from other agencies and working in partnership with them.

Introduction

This chapter looks at how the need for sensory awareness in practice has increased due to people living longer. A report by SCIE (2007a) highlighted the risks that deafblind people are exposed to. The report discusses combined sight and hearing loss leading to a higher risk of vulnerability, isolation and depression. We will consider how these risks are emulated or reproduced when addressing all sensory needs so therefore will be critically reflecting upon loss and bereavement in relation to sensory need. We will also be exploring how the ethical frameworks of deontology and utilitarianism are useful tools in social work practice. We will consider the care management role and the challenges that have arisen from developments in the ways that social care is delivered, the impact it has on service users and workers (Carey, 2003; Postle, 2002; DoH, 2003, 2005, 2007; Cabinet Office, 2005). Adult assessment frameworks will be examined, as understanding these is essential to individualise adult social care provision. Legislative themes will be interwoven throughout the chapter.

A further report by SCIE (2007b) highlighted that a large number of people who have dual sensory loss develop it after the age of 60, with people often living beyond the age of 85 years. The report, which focused on dual sensory impairment or deafblindness, also highlighted the risks that deafblind people are exposed to such as a higher risk of vulnerability, isolation and depression. While the focus of the report was on deafblindness, it could be argued that as there are around 2 million people in the UK with a sight problem (RNIB) and around 9 million Deaf/deaf/deafened and hard of hearing people in the UK (RNID), potential risks such as these could apply to any individual with a sensory need.

Unfortunately the complexities of deafblindness, sight impairment, Deafness, deafness or hearing impairment are often little understood by staff in adult services as it could be argued that there is an expectation that the loss of sight and/or hearing is a natural part of the aging process. Most people with sensory loss experience significant life impact and that is why sensory awareness is fundamental to good practice. Although it is not possible for every practitioner to have specialist sensory skills or knowledge, it is important to be aware that most people can draw on previous sensory experience, personal/familial experience and specialist organisational knowledge such as SENSE, Deafblind UK (deafblind), BDA, RNID (deafness) and RNIB (blindness). Often these specialist organisations are willing and able to assist with specialist information, advice and support when we are working with a person who has a sensory need. For example, the RNID (available at www.rnid.org.uk) offer free confidential and impartial information on a range of subjects including tinnitus, employment, equipment, legislation and benefits, as well as many issues relating to deafness, tinnitus and hearing loss.

As highlighted in the SCIE (2007b) report, people who experience both sight and hearing loss have to cope with the complexities of dual sensory loss, since the loss of one sense cannot compensate for the loss of the other. Therefore, things other people take for granted pose a significant risk for a person who is deafblind (SENSE, 2007).

CASE STUDY

Miles was born deaf, but became severely partially sighted in his 60s. Miles has always been active and his hobbies included walking and rambling. The road near his home is busy and often presents difficulties for him. If Miles was blind, he could still hear the beep of a pedestrian crossing in order to cross safely. If he was Deaf/deaf he could see the flashing green man. As Miles is deafblind he can neither hear the beep nor see the flashing green man. The loss of both senses creates unique complexities for Miles.

Parker and Bradley highlight that *a social work assessment is a focused collation, analysis and synthesis of relevant collected data pertaining to the presenting problem and identified needs* (2007, p13).

ACTIVITY *4.1*

Look at the case study of Miles together with Parker and Bradley's assessment description. How would you assess Miles to prevent risk of vulnerability, isolation and depression? Would you contact any specialist organisations to assist you in your assessment, planning and intervention?

Comment

Your assessment may have identified that as Miles's sensory need has now changed, the focus of your assessment needs to change also. This task is achieved by homing in on Miles's individual specific sensory needs. For example, to prevent risk of vulnerability, isolation and depression, Miles may benefit from a referral to the local sensory services team for him to be referred for a communicator guide. This would enable him to be empowered as he would be in a position to access information, leisure services and access appropriate communication. To illustrate, the communicator guide may accompany Miles to his rambling club, facilitate communication and ensure that Miles is aware of updates/information. Additionally, your assessment may have identified that Miles may benefit from specialist information and knowledge of organisations such as SENSE or Deafblind UK. You could access these and use them in your intervention while empowering Miles to access them himself.

Critical reflection on the complexities of Miles's situation enables us to be empathic in our social work practice and thus practise holistically, individually and effectively. A further factor that has relevance to our practice in working with people with sensory need is that of bereavement and loss. In the next section the significance of understanding bereavement and loss in relation to sensory need will be considered.

Bereavement and loss

ACTIVITY *4.2*

To begin, list your own perceptions of loss. Critically reflect on what loss means to you as an individual. Write down times in your own life when you feel you have experienced loss.

Comment

Understanding loss is essential to disability because it is a key aspect of social work (Currer, 2007). However, until we understand our own perceptions of loss, it is difficult to be empathic to others. Loss experienced by service users, their families and carers should always be addressed to endeavour to achieve best practice and obtain the best outcome

(Currer, 2007). It is a requirement within the Codes of Practice (GSCC, 2001) that we engage in ongoing professional development; part of this is critical reflection on bereavement and loss in relation to disability or sensory needs as this helps to develop empathic, effective practice.

Incorporating models and theories of loss is invaluable in social work practice. We shall be exploring ways for understanding loss and bereavement in detail in Chapter 6, but we shall discuss two important models here, a classic model and a more recent model. The first model is the classic model developed by Kübler-Ross (1970), who conducted a well-known observational study of people who had received a terminal diagnosis. Although originally intended as a study on the process of dying, it has been known as a model for understanding grief (Currer, 2007). The five stages of grief that were identified begin with the stage of denial, in which a common reaction to bad news is disbelief, a sense that it cannot be true. In Kübler-Ross's model, this is followed by the second stage of anger, in which people may feel *How can this happen?* or *Why me?* Commonly, people may feel that someone must be blamed. The third stage is bargaining, which is characterised by a sense of wanting to negotiate with fate some control, e.g. living until a specific event, such as a wedding or the birth of a grandchild. This is followed by the fourth stage, depression, in which the person begins to accept the reality of the loss and this can lead to sadness and possibly guilt and unworthiness. The final stage in the model is acceptance, in which happiness and contentment may not be experienced, but a sense of resolution marks the end of active struggle (Currer, 2007).

Kübler-Ross's model has been criticised for being overly prescriptive and more recent models have been influenced by sociological theories which focus on our sense of identity and how it is constructed. The second model we shall look at comes from this tradition and is the *new model of grief* (Walter, 1996), which argues that the purpose of grief is to sustain the link with the lost person rather than to 'move on' (Currer, 2007, p68). Walter (1996) highlights the views of many bereaved people that they do not want to move on from their loved one. The experience of loss means that the nature of the bond has to change but it is a matter of relocating the loved one rather than leaving them behind.

Whichever model you find helpful, it is important to remember that they are not meant as rigid frameworks. All research including Kübler-Ross's and Walter's is based on their views, perceptions and experiences; thus it is important to be specific about research that underpins theoretical frameworks and ensure that we treat each person individually and not be theoretically inflexible.

It could be argued that loss can be viewed from two perspectives: that of finite loss, which is the type of loss used to describe death, and non-finite loss, for example, disability, chronic illness, infertility, divorce, adoption and sensory loss (Bruce and Shultz, 2001; Currer, 2007). Sensory loss could be perceived as finite loss in terms of the sense, be it sight, sound, touch, smell, being lost and unable to be regained. However, for the purpose of this section we will be focusing on non-finite loss, i.e. grief that is ongoing and altering as life constantly falls short of expectations (Collins, 2008; Bruce and Shultz, 2001).

It could be argued that non-finite loss aptly describes sensory loss as often sensory loss will not be stable but will be progressive, often leading to progressive deterioration.

Sensory loss can affect numerous aspects of an individual's life. It can affect the person emotionally, physically, mentally and psychologically. It can affect their independence, socialisation, job prospects, learning opportunities, communication, familial interaction and so on. Critically reflecting on the extensive areas of life that sensory loss encompasses, it is not surprising that the person experiencing sensory loss may have ongoing or non-finite feelings of loss, bereavement and grief. It is therefore essential for practitioners not only to understand the impact of sensory loss, but also to engage in empathic practice by acknowledging and legitimising the individual's feelings of loss to enable them to adapt to non-finite loss. Practising in this way can preserve identity, restore control and honour the significance of loss (Bruce and Shultz, 2001).

CASE STUDY

Beatrice has always been passionate about painting and specialised in watercolours. She worked as an artist for the last 20 years of her working life prior to her recent retirement and was extremely successful. Beatrice had recently begun to find that she could not see to paint as well as she used to. Upon visiting the ophthalmologist she was diagnosed with retinitis pigmentosa. While Beatrice now understands the reasons for her inability to paint as well as she used to, the eye condition that she has means that she has progressive degeneration of the retina, resulting in night blindness and decreased peripheral vision. Beatrice is devastated.

ACTIVITY 4.3

Critically analyse Beatrice's situation. Use theoretical concepts in relation to loss and bereavement, knowledge of the eye condition she experiences, transferable social work skills and empathy. How could you preserve Beatrice's identity, restore her control and honour the significance of her loss?

Comment

While a practitioner may do their best to provide holistic service provision and support to a person who has a sensory loss, it is also essential to remember that not all service users will respond the same. A person's ability to work with their sensory loss will depend on many aspects. It could depend on whether the person was born sighted and hearing and later acquired sensory loss; if they were born deaf and later became sight impaired or severely sight impaired; or if the person was born sighted and later became deaf, deafened or hard of hearing. It can depend on individual unique personality and their perception of their sensory loss. It can also be impacted by their environment, services available and support (family, friends, carers, statutory, voluntary and independent). It may be that people need time to deal with their loss or counselling to support them. You may even find that people will isolate themselves and refuse to accept any form of support or assistance. While the social work role of assessment is to collate and study information, it is also important to remember that assessments are not just fact-finding missions but represent a *joint construction of a narrative or story between social worker and service user* (Parker and Bradley, 2007, p16). Parker and Bradley (2007) further highlight that social work has to be *sensitive and demonstrate an ability to be able to value the uniqueness of each individual assessed* (p15). This uniqueness is illustrated by the fact that not all people will consider themselves to have a sensory loss.

As previously discussed, within the deaf community there is a division of thought with regard to the issue of deafness being classified as sensory loss. Someone who has acquired deafness as a result of meningitis, accident or trauma would most likely consider themselves to have sensory loss (Hearing Concern, 2007). However, some 'D' Deaf people take a politicised stance on deafness and do not consider themselves to have a sensory loss (Peters, 2000). Sacks (1991) describes Deaf people who have been part of a Deaf community as a linguistic minority with their own culture and history. These perceptions once again highlight the significance of respect for diversity and individuality.

As already highlighted in previous chapters, theoretical concepts can be useful tools when working in a human services profession (Banks, 2006). Next, we will consider the role theoretical ethical frameworks can play in assessment and intervention.

Ethics

Ethical dilemmas can arise within our work. In order to critically analyse these we will next define what an ethical dilemma actually is, embrace critical thinking when approaching these dilemmas and explore the theoretical ethical frameworks of deontology and utilitarianism to support us in unravelling them.

To begin, we will define 'ethical dilemma'. Hugman highlights ethical thoughts as *the process by which we identify right and good and work out how we may best achieve these* (Hugman, 2003, p5). Thompson (1996, p274) defines dilemma as *a state of indecision between two alternatives*.

Wilks (2005) argues that social workers commonly face the issue of when to restrict choices of service users because issues *around self-determination are conceived as being about principles in conflict or tension but by being reflexive, anti-oppressive and anti-discriminatory in our practice these dilemmas can be addressed* (Wilks, 2005, p1257). Wilks (2005) further talks about the concept of observing the movie as well as the snapshot. This often refers to multiple layers of complexity (Banks, 2006). This can include agency constraints, personal values, service user values/views, views of partners, siblings, parents, children, carers and so on.

To help us understand how ethical frameworks can be useful in our work we will be using the case study of Parveen. We will use this case study throughout this section, critically exploring and analysing each stage to help us to determine intervention that contributes to best practice.

CASE STUDY

Parveen is deafblind and has a learning disability. Now that Parveen is 21 she has decided that she no longer wants to live with her parents. She wants to live on her own and control her own money. Parveen's parents vocalised their concerns regarding this. They do not feel that it would be safe for Parveen to live alone or control her own finances.

ACTIVITY 4.4

Look at the case of Parveen. Use critical thinking activities to explore your own social work values in relation to Parveen's predicament. Remember critical thinking activities include:

- *decision-making and planning, use of discretion;*

- *responsibility; risk assessment;*

- *seeking out and taking proper account of all stakeholders' input;*

- *thinking through implications;*

- *predicting possible outcomes but planning for alternatives (Brown and Rutter, 2006, p39).*

Comment

Flynn and Saleem (1986) highlight that lack of autonomy for people with intellectual difficulties is typical. While parental actions may be due to overprotectiveness (Oliver and Sapey, 2006) and well-meaning, sometimes it is hard for the carer or parent to move a person with a disability towards independence.

Parveen's dilemma illustrates the ethical realisation that problems are not always solvable (Banks, 2006). As we will explore later in this chapter, limited agency resources (Carey, 2003) and processes dominated by agency agendas (Richards, 2000) can make it challenging to meet the needs of the service user. This may highlight further ethical conflicts in deciding whether the *increasingly rationed and procedurally based focus of care management work is in the best interests of the service user* (Parrott, 2007, p5).

Sometimes it can be difficult to balance personal views, choice, risk and agency agenda. We may hold the personal belief that Parveen has the right to choice/autonomy (Heenan, 2005). Professionally, we are duty-bound to balance choice/risk (Parrott, 2007); to implement professional standards (GSCC, 2001) and critically reflect on how to approach this ethical dilemma (Fook and Askeland, 2007). The role of the care manager/social worker is complex as in addition we also have to comply with legislation, government guidance and initiatives.

To enable us to understand how the theoretical frameworks of deontology and utilitarianism can be useful tools when exploring ethical dilemmas, we first need to understand what these theoretical concepts entail.

Deontology

The word 'deontology' derives from the Greek words for duty (*deon*) and science or study of (*logos*). In contemporary moral philosophy, deontology is a theory regarding which choices are morally required, forbidden or permitted. To explain, this means that the concept of deontology could be described as a moral theory that could be used to guide and influence the choices that we make in practice.

The deontological concepts emphasise duty as the basis of moral value. This means that deontological theory focuses on right over good. A well-known deontological theorist was Immanuel Kant (1724–1804). Kant's theory was that the source of moral duty is pure reason itself, which means that there is a moral duty to be respected and honoured. The deontological theory states that people should adhere to their obligations and duties. This means a person will follow his or her obligations to another individual or society because upholding one's duty is what is considered ethically correct. A deontologist's practice would be consistent as it would be based on the individual's set of duties that he or she imposes on him/herself. An interesting concept of this theory is that the deontologist can perform an act of supererogation. This means that the deontologist would exceed their self-imposed duties. To illustrate, a sky-diving instructor is doing a plane jump with her student. Following the jump, both parachutes fail to open. The act of supererogation would mean that the instructor, by exceeding her self-imposed duty, would put herself in a position so she would absorb the impact of the landing to save the student.

The deontologist would see the duty or obligation to take the right action as all important even if the consequences of the actions are disastrous. While it could be argued that the theory of deontology is attributed with many positive aspects, it could also be critiqued that there may be no rationale or logical basis for an individual deciding his/her duty (Banks, 2005; Parrott, 2007).

Utilitarianism

The ethical theory of utilitarianism is based on the ability to predict the consequences of action and the concept of doing the greatest good for the greatest number.

There are two aspects of utilitarianism: act utilitarianism and rule utilitarianism. Act utilitarianism requires us to perform an 'act' that would be to the greatest good of the greatest number regardless of conflicting personal feelings or conflicting laws. Rule utilitarianism still works to the greatest good for the greatest number but instead adheres to the law and is concerned about justice and fairness. It could be argued that a critique of utilitarianism is that while you can draw on life experience it is not possible to predict the consequences of actions accurately and thus a decision that could benefit the greatest good for the greatest number on one occasion could alter as consequences change. To illustrate: a group of people on an island elect someone from among themselves to take charge and set up rules where they can share things out equally, look out for each other and live harmoniously together. It appears this decision is for the greatest good of the greatest number. However, the elected person gets carried away with their position and starts to dictate and force things through for their own selfish gain. The rules they make are no longer to the greatest good for the greatest number and democracy turns to dictatorship.

The original utilitarian action was intended to be beneficial for the greatest good of the greatest number. Is this still the case? It could be argued that as the consequences could not be predicted, so the outcome of the action could not be predicted either, thus highlighting flaws in the theory of utilitarianism. As with all theoretical concepts we need to critically analyse the implications for our practice. Critical analysis of our practice requires conscious action on our part, as it involves *exploring feelings, actions, decisions linking theory to practice and challenging or questioning underlying knowledge and assumptions* (Brown and Rutter, 2006, p19).

Hugman (2003) argues that professional ethics in social work have often been embroiled in a debate between deontological and utilitarian approaches. To illustrate, social workers carry out a duty (deontological); however, every decision affects consequences (utilitarian).

Returning to the case study of Parveen, she wanted personal financial control and independent living while her parents raised concerns. We have explored the theoretical frameworks of deontology and utilitarianism, so now let us look at how these theories can be applied to practice.

ACTIVITY 4.5

From a deontological *theoretical framework:*

- *critically analyse whether you feel that it is your duty as Parveen's care manager to ensure her 'rights are respected' (GSCC code 4) concurrently 'seeking to ensure her behaviour does not harm her' (GSCC code 4);*

- *critically reflect on what would happen if Parveen mismanaged her finances and was not able to purchase food, clothing or shelter;*

- *critically explore your own values and beliefs on how you feel about Parveen's rights to autonomy.*

Comment

Deontological theory states that people should adhere to obligations and duties when analysing an ethical dilemma. However, as we have seen, it could be argued that duty recognition can be complicated in itself as it involves a balancing act. It takes into account agency viewpoint low resources and managerialistic agency constraints (Carey, 2003), which mean issues need resolving swiftly. It expects respect for service user autonomy and recognition of users' rights to freely make their own decisions and choices while balancing this with risk (Osmo and Landau, 2006), adherence to GSCC (2001) guidance and so on.

We will now explore Parveen's situation from a utilitarian perspective. Applying the principle of the greatest good for the greatest numbers may influence the decision in favour of the parents. However, this may not promote justice and fairness towards Parveen, who has rights to choice/autonomy over her finances and life choices (DoH, 2001). Utilitarianism considers the consequences of Parveen self-managing her finances. Parveen may mismanage her money and be unable to fend for herself. *Traditionally, utilitarianism has considered that any decision should account for the balance of pleasure over pain* (Parrott, 2007, p52). Parveen's dilemma needs balance to enable her to be empowered (Thompson, 1998) while preventing risk (GSCC, 2001).

ACTIVITY 4.6

Look at Parveen's situation from a utilitarian theoretical framework and develop a plan to enable Parveen to have choice and autonomy while keeping her safe. (Parrott, 2007)

Comment

A utilitarian perspective may suggest developing guidelines for Parveen ensuring she has appropriate housing, is able to pay for her food/shelter/clothing first, is appropriately supported and then has financial choice/autonomy after the essentials are paid for (Parrott, 2007). This would uphold the principles of 'justice and fairness', detrimental consequences could be minimised and the principle of the greatest good for the greatest number could be applied.

As briefly highlighted earlier, governmental development has impacted on adult social care services, for the service user, their families/carers and the worker. Next we will explore the care management role and the challenges it presents.

Care management

In adult services, social workers are referred to as either social workers or care managers. Care management was introduced following the introduction of the National Health Service and Community Care Act (NHS and CCA) 1990. Prior to the introduction of this Act, there had been some criticisms of the way that social care for older adults was delivered (for more information see Parker and Bradley, 2007, p25). The blueprint for care management was outlined in the White Paper, *Caring for People* (DoH, 1989), the aims being to provide a framework for community care in the 1990s and in the future. However, as we will explore later in the chapter, sometimes busy care management environments are fraught with budgetary/time constraints and procedural agency agendas (Postle, 2002; Carey, 2003). In April 1993, the NHS and CCA 1990 was implemented and *qualified social workers were appointed as care managers* (Parker and Bradley, 2007, p25). Under section 47 of the NHS and CCA 1990, local authorities now had a duty to assess. However, this is not to be confused with a duty to provide. Assessments became more needs-focused and provision of care and services was to be made with regard to the level of need the service user required instead of fitting the service user into care and services that were available. Within a sensory working environment this is where creative care management can be useful. Direct work that does not involve costings or funding requirements can be used to provide a service.

CASE STUDY

Sam is profoundly deaf and lives in a nursing home. Staff members in the home have intimated that Sam likes to isolate himself and that he is often depressed. Sam has never been assertive, has always been shy, so he just sits in his room, on his own. The care manager Lucy has been allocated to Sam to review his care needs. While talking to Sam, Lucy soon realised that while Sam can't communicate in noisy, overcrowded environments, he can lipread, and thus can communicate on a one-to-one basis. Lucy asks Sam if he likes games, he says he loved to play dominoes, but doesn't do it now. Lucy speaks to the activities organiser, David, in the nursing home, explaining that Sam doesn't want to be isolated, but is just a bit shy. Lucy also explains that Sam can communicate well on a one-to-one basis, if he is facing the person and can read their lips. Lucy gives David a few tips on communicating with a profoundly deaf person, like ensuring that you are facing the person when you speak, touching their hand to get their attention and ensuring the person being lipread is in a well-lit area. David then arranges for Sam to play dominoes with one of the other residents.

ACTIVITY **1.1**

Critically reflect on how Sam may have been feeling prior to the care manager's intervention. How do you think Sam would have felt after having contact with one of the other residents, doing something he enjoyed? Picture yourself as a creative care manager; can you think of any other non-cost activities or interventions that could benefit Sam?

Comment

Remember all the people we work with are autonomous, so may not want to follow up areas we source, but at least by being creative you are promoting the interests of the service users, empowering them and providing choice (GSCC, 2001). However, within the care management/social work role, challenges have arisen, and next we will consider some of these.

Social work/care management challenges

While there are many adult assessment frameworks, initiatives and guidance outlines (which we will explore later in this section) that impact on the delivery of social care, it could equally be argued that busy care management environments which are fraught with budgetary/time constraints, and also procedural agency agendas also impact on the actual service provision.

To illustrate, we will explore the Department of Health guidance entitled *Social care for deafblind children and adults* (2001). Under Section 7 of the Local Authority Social Services Act 1970, this guidance placed new duties on local authorities and gave new rights to deafblind people. This guidance meant that local authorities had to:

- identify, make contact with and keep a record of deafblind people;

- ensure that assessments are carried out by a specifically trained person/team;

- ensure that appropriate services are provided;

- provide one-to-one support by communicator guides who provide assistance with correspondence, telephone calls, reading newspapers, escorting on shopping trips, appointments (such as hospital, GP, hairdresser) social engagements, cultural or recreational activities or conversations at home to relieve isolation (appendix 2);

- provide information in accessible formats;

- make sure that senior management have overall responsibility.

While this document is guidance, not legislation, if local authorities fail to adhere to this guidance they can be subject to judicial review. This guidance therefore highlighted a need for social workers/care managers to be deafblind aware.

The implication for social work practice is that under the Local Authority Social Services Act 1970 (s.7) older people's services have a responsibility to address the issue of dual sensory need. However, when addressing the pressures and constraints placed on care managers (Carey, 2003), it is unlikely sensory needs will be placed as a priority when assessing areas of need. Carey (2003) questions whether need is even being partially met (Carey, 2003, p121) and continues by saying *care managers are rarely able to utilise the skills that they develop during the Diploma in Social Work course. Frustration is felt on behalf of staff in the area office who are now working under considerable strain, with little recognition to the consequences of continued deskilling of social work and retrenchment of what little remains in welfare* (Carey, 2003, p121). When looking at the stresses and pressures that social work/ care management staff are experiencing, does it seem logical that staff working in adult services will have the time, opportunity, energy or resources to address sensory issues?

Literature discussing issues faced in older people's services does not reflect positive implications for practice. Richards (2000) discusses attempts to understand the needs of older people becoming increasingly difficult when processes are dominated by agency agendas (Richards, 2000). Jones (2001) argues that social workers who work on the front line feel that their work has been *transformed and degraded* (Jones, 2001, p547), and continues to say that the *needs of the client are being largely ignored* (Jones, 2001, p547). When analysing these views it is not surprising that social workers/care managers do not have the time and resources to respond to additional needs that may arise for individuals. Postle (2002) discusses 'ambiguities and tensions in care managers' work', where *care managers are trying to reconcile spending more time on paperwork and computer work with having less time for making and working within relationships with people* (Postle, 2002, p335). Postle (2002) further expands that this way of working increases stress levels and results in staffing problems, which affects the quality of service given to older people. Carey (2003) argues that a care management culture exists in social work which focuses on *care management practice being removed from definitions of social work as regards the influence of values and theories as they are defined in text books, academic papers or in college and university departments that teach social work* (Carey, 2003, p122). Carey continues to argue that this care management culture has developed in older people's services due to changes exacerbated by the NHS and Community Care Act 1990. Carey talks about social work becoming care management and the focus changing to a manageralistic assessment process and arranging packages of care as opposed to autonomous, therapeutic, relational social work (Carey, 2003).

This poses the question: do workers have time to recognise and subsequently address sensory issues? Postle (2002) argues that *it is questionable how far care management practice is currently meeting older people's needs* (Postle, 2002, p348) and as a large proportion of adults with sensory needs are over 65 years this would include this client group. It could be argued that older people's services are not sensory aware because of the environmental barriers imposed upon them due to the care management system of *working under strain* (Carey, 2003, p121). However, while it is unarguable that the care management/ social work role has many challenges to overcome, as highlighted in the case study of Sam, creative practice can really benefit the people we work with. Drawing on the sensory experience we have, or using specialist organisations to influence our assessment and intervention, can be invaluable in our practice.

Within adult social care there are a number of assessment frameworks available to social workers/care managers. In order to provide effective service delivery we need to understand them, so in the next section we will consider some of these.

Adult assessment frameworks

A number of government initiatives have contributed to a variety of adult assessment frameworks. In order to creatively use these initiatives to benefit people with sensory needs it is essential to understand what is available. In this section in chronology by year order, we will explore:

- *Direct Payments* (DPs, 1996);

- *No Secrets* (DoH, 2000);

- *Valuing People* (DoH, 2001);

- *Autistic Spectrum Consultation* (DoH, 2009);

- *National Services Framework for Older People* (DoH, 2001);

- *Fair Access to Care Services* (FACS, 2003);

- *The Prime Minister's Strategy Unit Report* (2005);

- *Personalised Budgets* (PB, 2005);

- *The Common Assessment Framework* (DCSF, 2006);

- *The Putting People First initiative* (DoH, 2007).

Direct Payments (1996)

The Community Care (Direct Payments) Act 1996 introduced direct payments. A pilot direct payments project subsequently began in rural Norfolk in 1997 to evaluate the outcome (Joseph Rowntree Foundation, 2009). According to Dawson (2000, p1) *direct payments have been heralded as a way for disabled people to gain more independence and control over their lives*. The aim of direct payments is to enable disabled people to have greater choice, autonomy and flexibility in care provision by giving individuals cash in lieu of social services provision of services. The service user can either choose care delivery themselves or request support in engaging services.

Direct payments can be made to a disabled person over the age of 16 years, to people with parental responsibility for disabled children (see Chapter 5) and to carers aged 16 or over in relation to care services (DoH, 2009). The initiative behind direct payments is to enable the service user to have greater participation in how their care is delivered. Since changes in the law, it is a duty for direct payments to be made.

The Joseph Rowntree Foundation supported the pilot project by funding a researcher to evaluate the project. The research findings revealed that:

- social workers are the gatekeeper to direct payment – most often the service user finds out about direct payment from the social worker;
- good practice is developed when the social services department and the social worker come from a perspective of the disabled person's competence rather than their incompetence and assessing the concepts of 'willing and able';
- in order for the scheme to be practical and workable, disabled people need to be involved in the introduction and operation of any scheme that directly affects their lives including direct payments.

Dawson (2000) also argues that the introduction of cash payments in lieu of social services provision can be highly complex for disabled people. However, within a sensory environment direct payments can be useful as they can be used creatively, for example, communication guide services could be purchased. However, following what now appears to be the successful implementation of direct payments and just as people have got used to the idea of direct payments, personalised budgets are introduced. We will explore personalised budgets a bit further later on in this section.

No Secrets (DoH, 2000)

> *This document gives guidance to local agencies that have a responsibility to investigate and take action when a vulnerable adult is believed to be suffering abuse. It offers a structure and content for the development of local inter-agency policies, procedures and joint protocols which will draw on good practice nationally and locally.*
>
> (DoH, 2000)

The guidance was a tool for developing multi-agency policies and procedures to protect vulnerable adults from abuse. The blueprint required local procedures to be set up to enable incidents of abuse of vulnerable adults and those with learning difficulties to be reported, investigated and acted upon. The setting up of this guidance led to greater awareness of the rights of vulnerable people and those with learning difficulties. This paper was also important for people with sensory needs as people with a sensory need may be vulnerable and /or physically, mentally or learning disabled.

It is important to note that as well as reporting an incident to the local authorities (adult services), incidents can also be reported to *police, the Commission for Social Care inspection (CSSI) ... or organisations concerned with protection from abuse. These include, Voice UK, the Ann Craft Trust, Respond ... and Mencap ...* (Williams, 2006, p107).

Valuing People (2001) and *Valuing People Now* (2009)

The four main principles of the *Valuing People* White Paper (DoH, 2001) are:

- rights;

- independence;

- choice;

- inclusion.

The principal focus is on the fact that people with learning difficulties themselves, and representatives of their families/carers, were closely involved in the fundamental work behind the paper (Williams, 2006). A service user advisory group was set up, comprising members of self-advocacy groups with a small group of supporters to enable the people with learning difficulties' views to be expressed (Williams, 2006). The primary difference was that people with learning difficulties were now involved in service provision that directly affected them personally.

Valuing People Now (January 2009) is a three-year strategy that has been launched cross-government. The initiative is for a plan to be set out for people with learning disabilities. The plan sets out governance structure and actions, with timescales and responsibilities to support people with learning difficulties.

A new national group has also been set up called the National Learning Disability Programme Board. It includes people from:

- the government;

- the national forum;

- the National Valuing Families Forum;

- voluntary organisations.

Additionally, there will also be a new group in every region called the Regional Learning Disability Programme Boards. These will include:

- people with learning disabilities themselves;

- families and carers.

Understanding the range of initiatives available is essential to individualisation of delivery provision, especially if the person with the learning difficulty also has a sensory need. Williams (2006) highlighted that people with learning difficulties experience more eyesight and hearing difficulties than the general population. Levey (1997) highlights that in a survey it was revealed that around 60 per cent of all people with learning difficulties have a sensory impairment. Often learning difficulty services provide services for adults with

Asperger syndrome or autism. While we will briefly explore autism and Asperger syndrome in this section, we will continue to explore it in more depth in the next section. Autism involves difficulties in understanding in areas of relationship and emotion which some-times results in unique behaviours. These behaviours can be in the form of unusual or obsessional behaviours. People with Asperger syndrome may find it harder to read signals that most people take for granted. It may also be more difficult for them to communicate (see National Autistic Society website at www.nas.org.uk. Williams (2006) recommends the novel *The Curious Incident of the Dog in the Night-time* by Mark Haddon (2003) as it gives an impression of what autism is like.

CASE STUDY

Aadarshini is 19 years old and was born partially sighted, hard of hearing and is on the autis-tic spectrum disorder. Aadarshini's hearing has started to deteriorate and the GP advises that a hearing test is required to establish the level of loss, in order to enable hearing aid provi-sion. However, Aadarshini has never liked anyone to touch her ears. She exhibits extreme challenging behaviour if anyone even touches her ears accidentally.

ACTIVITY 4.8

Critically reflect on how Aadarshini's disabilities impact on sensory equipment provi-sion. If she is unable to have her ears touched, how is the hearing test to be carried out? How is the mould for the hearing aid to be obtained? How is the hearing aid going to be fitted? Once the hearing aid is issued, how will it be put in each morning, removed each night and regularly removed for general maintenance, e.g. tube cleaning, battery changing etc.?

Comment

This case study of Aadarshini highlights that additional disabilities intensify the impact of sensory disabilities. Sometimes equipment, adaptations or communication that can be used to enhance sensory need may not be able to be used if a person has multiple disabili-ties. Sensory needs can be in additional to physical, mental health or learning difficulties, thus highlighting that each person we work with who has a sensory need, should be treated as a unique individual and why understanding assessment frameworks and guid-ance is essential. Next we will explore the Autistic Spectrum Consultation.

Autistic Spectrum Consultation (DoH, 2009)

Having briefly discussed autism and Asperger syndrome in the previous section, we will now explore it in more depth. The National Autistic Society describes autism as a life-long developmental disability which affects individuals with social communication, social interaction and social imagination. Additionally a person with autism can experience sen-sory needs not only in connection with sight and sound but also taste (dysgeusia), touch and smell (anosmia). People with autism most likely will not look different visually from those who do not have autism. However, often they like fixed routines and can also have associated needs such as learning difficulties, epilepsy, ADHD and dyspraxia. Asperger syndrome is a form of autism in which people may have difficulties with social communication, interaction and imagination and dyslexia. However, this is manifested in a milder form and many people with Asperger syndrome lead full lives (for more information see www.nas.org.uk/asperger). Before considering the government initiatives with regard to autistic spectrum consultation we will briefly explore how the three areas of social communication, social interaction and social imagination affect people with autism (for more information see www.nas.org.uk/autism).

Social communication affects verbal and non-verbal communication and often people with autism will take things very literally, for example with jokes, phrases, sayings and idioms. An example of this is the phrase 'raining cats and dogs', which while meaning that it is raining heavily may be taken literally by a person with autism. Some people who experience autism do not use verbal communication and may use sign language or visual symbols. As highlighted earlier in the book, much of communication is accidental learning, when someone has a sensory need and is not exposed to the idiosyncrasies of the English language, so again phrases, sayings and idioms may be taken literally. This combination of autism and sensory need can significantly increase complexity of need for an individual.

Social interaction affects people with autism and often they have difficulty recognising, controlling and expressing their own emotions. Additionally, they often find it hard to interact with others as they do not recognise the emotional need of others. People with autism often do not learn the unwritten rules when it comes to social interactional codes of conduct. For example, they may stand too close or intercept with inappropriate conversation on an inappropriate topic. As people with autism find it more difficult to form friendships, they may often prefer to spend time alone.

Difficulties with social imagination mean that people with autism find it difficult to understand and envisage other people's behaviour, thoughts and feelings. They may not adapt to unfamiliar surroundings and may even get lost if they are in an area they do not know. They may also not understand the concept of danger and veer into busy roads or go somewhere with another individual who presents a danger to them. Another way an autistic person's social imagination difficulties may manifest themselves are in repetitive re-enactment of what they see. For example, they may engage in repetitive re-enactment behaviour of a TV programme they have seen. All of these difficulties make it harder for people with autism to make plans for their future and therefore highlight the need for tailor-made services to empower people to reach their full potential.

Having briefly considered the impact of autism on a person, we will now consider the *Autistic Spectrum Consultation* (DoH, 2009). There are various forms of terminology used to describe a person who is on the autistic spectrum; these include autistic spectrum disorder, autistic spectrum difference, neuro-diversity and autistic spectrum condition. The Department of Health for the purpose of their consultation have used the term Autistic Spectrum Condition (ASC).

It has now been recognised that people with ASC have need of specifically targeted services to enable them to live their lives to their fullest potential. Currently, it could be argued that service provision is inadequate to meet specific need requirements of people with ASC.

The purpose of the consultation is to have the appropriate evidence base to submit proposals that will meet the needs of people with ASC. As the severity and behaviours of people with ASC vary significantly it is imperative that specific information is collated to enable appropriate services to be provided. Some people with ASC may function relatively well on a day-day-basis, other people will need lifelong specialist support.

The aim of the consultation is to discuss openly with people who understand and specialise in ASC and collate comprehensive data to improve service provision and meet need. Where appropriate services are provided a person with ASC can have the opportunities to reach their full personal potential. However, where a person is unsupported disastrous consequences can arise. Furthermore, the consultation is aiming to ensure equity of access to provision of goods and services, therefore comments are invited on this too.

The Department of Health's Autistic Spectrum Consultation (DoH, 2009) identifies five key areas.

1. Helping people where they live (both at home and with their day-to-day activities).

2. Making health care better.

3. Letting people with autism choose the services and support they need.

4. Helping people like doctors, social workers, teachers, the police, housing officers and other professionals understand more about autism.

5. Helping people with autism get jobs, training and benefits.

(For more information, see: www.adultautismstrategy.dialoguebydesign.net/)

The consultation outline highlights that the eventual plan will be called the *Adult Autism Strategy*. Next we will explore the *National Services Framework for Older People*.

National Service Framework (NSF) *for Older People* (2001)

As highlighted earlier, as people are getting older, more people will be affected by sensory loss. That is why developments such as the *National Service Framework* (NSF) for older people are essential to our practice. An NSF for Older People (DoH, 2001) was established to look at the problems older people face in receiving care in order to deliver higher-quality services. The key standards that underpin the Framework include plans to eradicate age discrimination and to support person-centred care with newly integrated services. Intermediate care was developed at home or in care settings, while general hospital care delivery was to be delivered by the appropriate hospital staff. The NHS also took action on stroke prevention, in the promotion of health and active life and on a reduction in the number of falls for older people. The aim of the NSF was also to integrate mental health services for older people.

However, it could be argued that the NSF initiative is ideological in its agenda because in practice the reality can sometimes be different (Crawford and Walker, 2007). One of the themes the NSF focuses on is *respecting the individual*, but this may not be the case if the worker is not sensory aware and thus is unaware of an individual's need. As already highlighted, sensory need is not always visible and thus can go unnoticed.

CASE STUDY

Gregor is in a nursing home and does not have any family. He has been there for six months. Gregor's home introduction was carried out by a care manager who has now left. A care manager named Nigel has now been allocated the case. Prior to working for the local authority, Nigel worked for SENSE. His knowledge and awareness of deafblindness are extensive. During the review, a staff member states that, while Gregor is no trouble, he is always so miserable. He never smiles or communicates. Nigel goes in to visit Gregor and as he is deafblind-aware, he asks the staff if Gregor has sight and hearing difficulties. They respond that they do not know as he refuses to communicate. Nigel uses some of his communication skills, such as touching Gregor's hand to alert him of his presence. It soon becomes clear that Gregor is deafblind and Nigel is able to facilitate communication and advise the nursing home staff of some useful strategies for communicating with Gregor.

An important element of practising anti-oppressively and in an anti-discriminatory manner is to be aware of the needs of disabled people regardless of their age, ethnicity, class, gender, etc., and provide creative alternatives to combat oppression and discrimination. In older people's services creative practice combined with sensory awareness can contribute to addressing these issues. Next we will explore the complexities of *Fair Access to Care Services* (FACS).

Fair Access to Care Services Criteria (2003)

In order to understand how the *Fair Access to Care Services* (FACS) criteria affect people with sensory need, it is initially important to understand what it is, its purpose for adult social care and its impact on adult services. *Fair Access to Care Service* (FACS) criteria were introduced in 2003 (Department of Health) and were designed to provide guidance for local authorities to set a framework for eligibility criteria in adult social care. FACS does not apply to children as their assessment of need is addressed through legislation. The aim of FACS was to establish fairer and more consistent eligibility criteria across the country. This equality of assessment of need applied to adults irrespective of their age, ethnicity, culture, religion, etc. Under FACS criteria, local authorities are only permitted to have one eligibility criterion for all adult social care. While local authorities can set their own criteria threshold to identify which bands of need are eligible for support, the qualifying criterion is based on needs and risk to independence. However, each council needs to take account of their own budgetary constraints, the need to support those individuals most at risk, the quantity of individuals needing support and NHS agreements (DoH, 2003). Under FACS criteria there are four eligibility bands in relation to risk of independence. These are:

- critical risk to independence;
- substantial risk to independence;

- moderate risk to independence;
- low risk to independence.

When addressing the eligibility bands, local authorities will look at risk of independence in relation to various tasks such as:

- personal care or domestic routines;
- involvement in work, education and learning;
- social support systems and relationships;
- family and other social roles and responsibilities.

'Low' risk to independence, according to FACS, is defined as: an inability to carry out one or two personal care or domestic routines; one or two aspects of learning, education or work cannot be sustained; one or two social support systems or relationships cannot be sustained; one or two family and other social roles and responsibilities cannot be undertaken.

As with 'low' risk, 'moderate' risk covers the same risk of independence in relation to personal care or domestic routines; involvement in work, education and learning; social support systems and relationships; and family and other social roles and responsibilities, except in the case of moderate risk there would be several instances where there is an inability to carry out or sustain the routine.

For 'substantial' risk, an individual would not be able to maintain or sustain the majority of tasks. In the case of 'critical' risk to independence, it means life is, or will be, threatened; significant health problems have developed or will develop; there will be little or no choice over vital aspects of the immediate environment; serious abuse or neglect has occurred or will occur; and that there is an inability to carry out or sustain any of the tasks.

The essential difference with FACS criteria is that they identify the impact a need has on an individual's independence, as opposed to the cause of the need. It also emphasises the need to review and evaluate services.

While carrying out an assessment under FACS criteria the practitioner is required to focus on risk in relation to:

- autonomy and freedom to make choices;
- health and safety including freedom from all categories of abuse;
- ability to manage own personal and daily routines;
- involvement in family and community life.

When assessing sensory need, FACS criteria still require focus to be on issues of health and safety, autonomy, personal and daily living activities, and maintenance of social, leisure or family involvement as a person with sensory need could easily fall into a higher risk eligibility band if sensory issues are not addressed. For example, if technical equipment needed by a person with a sensory loss is not provided, they could become at risk of isolation or loss of independence. Alternatively, it could be argued that if the equipment is provided it can prevent risk of isolation or loss of independence.

CASE STUDY

Jayne is in her 80s. She no longer hears well and even though she has been assessed by the audiologist, she has no useful residual hearing and subsequently is not able to have the benefit of hearing aids. Jayne can communicate on a one-to-one basis with her friend Stella who lives next door, as they have been friends for years, and Jayne lipreads Stella really well. The problem is that Jayne cannot hear the doorbell any more to enable Stella to have access to her home. Stella doesn't want a key to Jayne's door as she herself is over 80 and a bit forgetful. Jayne feels very isolated and depressed.

ACTIVITY **4.9**

Look at the FACS criteria. Which level of need do you think is applicable in Jayne's case? Think about which band Jayne would fall into if the equipment is provided ... and then if it isn't.

Flexible use of FACS criteria in relation to sensory need can be essential in prevention of risk.

Comment

Jayne was assessed under FACS criteria and her needs were assessed. The care manager's assessment revealed that Jayne would be at moderate–substantial risk if technical equipment for sensory need was not provided. Jayne was therefore issued by her local authority with a portable flashing doorbell. She no longer feels isolated as she can now answer the door to Stella and they can have a nice chat together. FACS criteria have reduced Jayne's risk of need and prevented isolation and loss of independence

Other areas where FACS criteria can be used as a preventative method in cases of sensory need may be in the provision of a text phone (minicom), a fax, a pager system, vibrating smoke alarm, room loop, magnifying glass, a symbol cane, an interpreter, and so on.

While there are positives to the introduction of FACS, it could still be argued that it has not achieved its aim of establishing fairer and more consistent eligibility criteria across the country, as there are still variations between areas. This is highlighted when it appears that some councils are able to offer more services than others. These observations thus identify a need for ongoing improvements for services for disabled people and those with a sensory need.

The Prime Minister's Strategy Unit Report (2005)

The Prime Minister's Strategy Unit Report was issued in January 2005 (Cabinet Office, 2005) and is a radical report focused on transforming the life chances of disabled people. The final report of 'transforming life chances for disabled people' states that by 2025 disabled people should have a full opportunity and choice to improve their quality of life and be equal and respected members of society. This is a joint venture between the Department for Work and Pensions (DWP), Department for Education and Skills (DfES), Office of the Deputy Prime Minister (ODPM – now called the Department for Communities and Local Government – DCLG) and the Prime Minister's (PM) Strategy Unit Report. Four main areas are addressed.

- *Independent living* The aim of this venture is to ensure disabled people have support based on choice, empowerment and personal need. This support is to be provided through a major expansion of the direct payment scheme in the form of individual budgets.

- *Early years and family support* (this will be addressed in Chapter 5).

- *Transition to adulthood* To enable disabled young people to have appropriate opportunities and choices as they move from children's to adult services. This is addressed further in Chapter 5.

- *Employment* Early intervention support assisting disabled people to stay in touch with the labour market. The support would be to those seeking work, to enable them to be supported through ongoing personalised support and supporting the employers in key roles, but also providing security for disabled people who are unable to work.

The radical vision for the report is to set out actions to enable disabled people to be full participants in the economy and in society. The *Disability Discrimination Act 1995/2005* has contributed to delivering civil rights to disabled people, but it could be argued that there is still much work to be done (BCODP, 2009). The British Council Of Disabled People (BCODP) came into existence in 1981 when a few national groups managed by disabled people such as the Union of the Physically Impaired Against Segregation (UPIAS, 1976) came together to form a council. UPIAS was founded in 1972 when Paul Hunt (who at the time lived in an institution) wrote a letter to the *Guardian* inviting a group of people to join him in tackling disability. The result was that the UPIAS become the first disability liberation group who placed disability in a social context in the UK.

The breakthrough for disability organisations came in 1981 when the United Nations declared it the International Year of Disabled People. It is the ongoing work of these and other disability-focused organisations and the understanding and the implementation of the social model of disability that is essential to furtherance of action to promote independence, choice, empowerment, respect and equality for disabled people. That is why papers such as *Valuing People* as explored earlier in this section, where service user involvement is critical, are so essential in the provision of service delivery. It also highlights that service user choice and autonomy are imperative. It could be argued that personalised budgets are a move towards greater choice and autonomy.

Personalised Budgets (DoH, 2005)

While people have now got used to the idea of direct payments (1996), some are not sure what a personalised budget (PB) is. According to the Department of Health (2009), an Individual Personalised Budget (IPB) is designed to provide individuals who currently receive services greater choice and control over their support arrangements. The government began PBs by piloting them in a number of local authorities. The aim is that PB will be rolled out over the country by 2012 (the aim of the new system is to amalgamate all relevant funding streams into PB) and that the service user has autonomy and choice on how to spend the budget. The service user can do this by themselves or with support. The IPB pilot project was a multi-government department initiative led by the Department of

Health working closely with the Department for Work and Pensions and the Department of Communities and Local Government. However, until the pilot is evaluated it is not possible to completely implement PB nationally.

The commitment to pilot individual budgets was made in the following documents.

- *Improving the Life Chances of Disabled People* (Strategy Unit, 2005).

- *Opportunity Age* (DWP, 2005).

- *Independence, Well-being and Choice* (DoH, 2005).

- *Our Health, Our Care, Our Say* (DoH, 2006).

The public response to both the Department of Health's Green Paper and White Paper were strongly in favour of developing models of care that place the individual at the centre of the social care delivery and that give them more choice and control over the care that they receive. The Department of Health promotes direct payments by promoting them more widely, in particular to groups that are currently excluded, and by developing and piloting the idea of individual budgets, including income streams other than councils' social care provision (DoH, 2005).

The DoH, the DCLG (formerly ODPM) and DWP have worked together to develop a starting model for individual budgets which will include some income streams including:

- council-provided social care services;

- Independent Living Fund;

- Supporting People;

- Disabled Facilities Grant;

- Integrated Community Equipment Services;

- Access to Work.

It could be argued that commitment to PBs and the extension of choice and control is reflected in the commitment in the *Our Health, Our Care, Our Say* White Paper (DoH, 2006) to establish a national network to support these developments.

However, it does remain to be seen what the impact of PBs will be overall. The Local Government Association of Adult Social Services on measuring council progress found that while some councils were providing PB's, not all councils had developed an integrated local area workforce strategy which would monitor workforce planning of statutory, independent and voluntary social care providers (ADASS, 2009). It could be argued that in the future, lack of workforce planning could impact on social workers and the role they carry out. Ruth Cartwright, Professional Officer for England, told the World Social Work Day conference in London (March 2009) that British Association of Social Work (BASW) members were reporting that the social work posts were being frozen by their authorities as they implemented personalisation. If this is to be the case, it will not only impact on the role of social workers, but each individual who receives a social care service. Next we will explore the *Common Assessment Framework for Adults*.

Common Assessment Framework for Adults (CAF – DoH, 2006/2009)

The original purpose of the *Common Assessment Framework* (DoH, 2006) was to *provide continuity of a person centred approach throughout adult life, geared towards self-determination and planning for independence*. One of the benefits proposed for this was a move towards a single assessment process (SAP), the idea behind SAP being that the assessment process for older people would be standardised to address personal care, physical well-being and mental health. Where multi-agency working was being performed, duplication would not be made of each other's assessment, thus promoting effective practice. There was to be a link between medical diagnosis and assessment, joint working for assessment and care planning, resulting in a single assessment summary where agreement was made on how to collect information, store and share it (Parker and Bradley, 2007).

However, since 2005 CAF has moved forward to consultation to improve information sharing around multi-agency assessments and care planning. The Department of Health (2009) launched a consultation which was of interest to the general public, commissioners of health, social care, wider community support services, the voluntary and independent sectors. The focus of the consultation was on improving the quality and efficiency of care and support through improvements in the sharing and use of information. The consultation focused on care and support for adults and on supporting the continued development of personalisation by assisting people to choose services more appropriate to their individual specific needs. As we can see from exploring the various initiatives, guidance outlines and assessment frameworks, adult service provision is still under development. Finally, in this section we will reflect on the *Putting People First* (2007) initiative.

Putting People First (DoH, 2007)

The *Putting People First* initiative was introduced in 2007. This government-led initiative was to embark on a three-year programme to personalise support for adults in social care involving collaboration between central and local government, the sector's professional leadership providers and the regulator. The aim of this radical reform of public services is to enable adults to have greater autonomy and choice in their own lives, enhanced confidence in higher-quality, safe services and opportunity to promote their own specific individual needs in relation to independence, well-being and dignity.

The importance of multi-agency collaboration is highlighted in this initiative. Trevithick (2005) highlights the importance of professionals maintaining contact. She also highlights the importance of service user choice as being integral to any problem-solving and decision-making processes that are carried out. Multi-agency working can be an asset for the service user, as each professional will come from their specific specialism, i.e. health, education, police and so on. However, when all professionals pool their resources, be it financial, intellectual or other resources, the service offered can be a holistic, tailor-made provision.

CASE STUDY

Elvira is 24 years old. Following a road traffic accident, she became blind. Up until that time Elvira had enjoyed her job as a proof reader. Since the accident Elvira has felt depressed and isolated. Richard, a social worker from the adult team in her borough, went to visit her to carry out an assessment of need under the National Health Service and Community Care Act 1990. While Elvira was coping with personal and domestic care, Richard noted that Elvira was uncommunicative and depressed. Richard discussed this with Elvira and she told him she had felt 'cut off from the world' since becoming blind, that she could not do her job and that her friends did not know what to say, or how, to treat her. Richard asked Elvira if she would be interested in learning something new; she said she would but how could she now that she was blind? Richard collaborated with the local college of further education to explore what courses they had for people with acquired blindness. The college had not worked with a blind person before, so advised Richard they would liaise with the Royal National Institute for Blind People (RNIB). All three agencies worked together to provide personalised college access.

ACTIVITY 4.10

Looking at the Putting People First *initiative, identify positive and negative aspects of multi-agency working. Critically reflect on the case study of Elvira. How do you feel multi-agency working provided a personalised service for her? Do you think the outcome would have been the same if collaborative working had not been embarked upon?*

Comment

As highlighted earlier, the aim of putting people first is to enable adults to have greater autonomy in their lives. Collaborative working contributes greatly to this process being successful. Elvira's circumstance had been radically changed but with creative thinking and collaborative working it was found that Elvira could still access college. The college consulted with RNIB and the local education authority to explore which voice-activated software would be appropriate to use in an educational setting. Software that converted text to voice and vice versa was sourced. Elvira was able to choose a course that interested her. To ensure that she had equal accessibility to the lectures, the course tutor had agreed that lectures could be audibly recorded for Elvira's personal reference. Essay preparation was enabled by using the voice-to-text software and the college provided a support worker to assist Elvira with any queries that arose. The result was that Elvira felt more integrated into society and increased in self-esteem and confidence. This could only be achieved by addressing Elvira's specific individual needs in relation to independence, well-being and dignity.

As highlighted in the case of Elvira, the Putting People First initiative, while a radical reform of public services, is able to enable adults to have greater autonomy and choice in their lives, promote enhanced confidence in higher-quality, safe services and opportunity to support the individual's own specific needs in relation to independence, well-being and dignity.

C H A P T E R   S U M M A R Y

To conclude, in this chapter we have explored the risks that people with sensory need are exposed to. We have highlighted how these risks can be minimised by understanding loss and bereavement, using theoretical ethical frameworks as tools for assessment and intervention, and understanding and implementing adult assessment frameworks, guidance and legislation in our practice. We have also considered the impact that adult social care delivery may have on the service user and the worker. As already highlighted, human services intervention is complex and that is why our practice needs continual development (GSCC, 2001), critical reflection, critical analysis and creativity.

FURTHER READING

Crawford, K and Walker, J (2007) *Social work and older people*. Exeter: Learning Matters.

Another supportive, educational and enjoyable book in the Transforming Social Work Practice series. This book will help students develop a distinctive focus on social work practice in the context of working with older people. It will enable readers to develop knowledge, skills and values that will enable them to promote and protect the individual and collective well-being of the older people with whom they work.

Parrott, L (2010) *Values and ethics in social work practice*. Second edition. Exeter: Learning Matters.

This book is part of the Transforming Social Work Practice series written specifically to support students on social work degree courses. Many students have little theoretical or practical experience of values and ethics in social work when they begin their studies. This book tackles that lack of knowledge by identifying current issues in applying ethical decisions to social work. These issues are then investigated further within an anti-discriminatory framework and against the background of the code of practice for social care workers and employers. Traditional value perspectives are clearly explained and current developments in virtue theory and ethics of care for social workers are also introduced.

Currer, C (2007) *Loss and social work*. Exeter: Learning Matters.

Again part of the Transforming Social Work Practice series. This book highlights the fact that social workers need to be aware of the impact of loss if they are to work effectively with service users at times of personal or family crisis. This book introduces and examines theoretical developments in relation to issues of change, loss and grieving, encouraging social workers to explore, through activities and case studies, how these may have relevance for their own practice. This is an area in which workers need to be aware of the potential impact of their own experience, and the book considers how practitioners may address this in a reflective manner.

Banks, S (2006) *Ethics and values in social work*. Third edition. Basingstoke: Palgrave Macmillan.

Written by a leading international authority, this book offers a clear and systematic account of professional ethics in relation to social work practice. It combines a sound grasp of theoretical issues with a sharp focus on the latest policy and practice.

Chapter 5

Sensory awareness in children and families

ACHIEVING A SOCIAL WORK DEGREE

This chapter will help to meet the following National Occupational Standards.

Key Role 1: Prepare for and work with individuals, families, carers, groups and communities to assess their needs and circumstances.

- Assess needs and options to recommend a course of action.

Key Role 3: Support individuals to represent their needs, views and circumstances.

- Advocate with, and on behalf of, individuals, families, carers, groups and communities.
- Assess whether you should act as the advocate for the individual, family, carer, group or community.
- Assist individuals, families, carers, groups and communities to access independent advocacy.
- Advocate for, and with, individuals, families, carers, groups and communities.

Key Role 4: Manage risk to individuals, families, carers, groups, communities, self and colleagues.

- Assess and manage risks to individuals, families, carers, groups and communities.
- Identify and assess the nature of the risk.

This chapter will also assist you to follow the GSCC (General Social Care Council) Codes of Practice for Social Care Workers.

GSCC Code 2: As a social care worker, you must strive to establish and maintain trust and confidence of service users and carers.

- Being reliable and dependable.

GSCC Code 4: As a social care worker, you must respect the rights of service users while seeking to ensure that their behaviour does not harm themselves or other people.

- Following risk assessment policies and procedures to assess whether the behaviour of service users presents a risk of harm to themselves or others.

GSCC Code 5: As a social care worker, you must uphold public trust and confidence in social care services.

In particular you must not:

- Abuse the trust of service users and carers or the access you have to personal information about them or to their property, home or workplace.

Introduction

This chapter will look at encouraging social workers in a child, family and education set-ting to develop sensory awareness in a professional context. This will be achieved by exploring sensory needs from child and parental perspectives and understanding the importance of individualised communication. You shall be invited to consider a life course perspective of how sensory needs may impact upon a child's vulnerability. We will examine assessment frameworks and how they can be informed by research findings relating to resilience and attachment theory. We shall discuss the importance of understanding culture, race and diversity with regard to sensory need. Finally, the roles of two key agencies, the General Social Care Council and the Children's Workforce Development Council, will be examined and the links with your professional development will be discussed.

Sensory needs from children's and parents' perspectives

When working with a parent or a child who has a sensory need, certain principles need to be considered.

- Always individualise the communication method used.

- Never assume that a child/parent can communicate in a particular method because they have a particular sensory need, e.g. assuming Deaf people use BSL, deafblind people use deafblind manual, and visually impaired people use voice/deafblind manual/block.

- Always obtain feedback to ensure you have been understood.

For the purpose of this section we will be mainly focusing on sensory needs from a parent's/child's perspective in relation to d/Deafness. However, the same principles need to be taken into account when working with people with visual impairment and deafblindness.

Deaf parents of hearing children

Working with a parent who has a sensory need requires attention to detail. Assumptions of a parent's understanding or use of a sensory-connected language should never be made. As has been highlighted consistently throughout this book, each person's sensory need will be unique and individual. To illustrate this we will look at the example of Robert.

CASE STUDY

Robert is a Deaf, 32-year-old white British man who uses sign language. A neighbour has contacted social services to report increasing noises of screaming and children crying coming from Robert's flat. The neighbour reports that Robert's children aged two and four years (both hearing) look dirty and unkempt. The neighbour is worried because while she has seen Robert and the two children, she has not seen Robert's wife Rose for at least a month. The neighbour fears that Robert and his wife have split up and that the children are being neglected.

ACTIVITY *5.1*

You are the duty social worker who has been asked to visit to carry out an initial assessment of the situation. You know that Robert is Deaf and that he uses sign language. What would be your next course of action? Would you consider booking an interpreter to take with you? What type of interpreter would you take?

Comment

You may think these are basic questions because after all, you know Robert is Deaf and uses sign language, so logically you will arrange for a sign language interpreter to be provided. However, just as with any other language, when a person has a sensory need, their linguistic acquisition can be varied. Robert may use sign language, but is it British Sign Language (BSL), Sign Supported English (SSE), Makaton or another communication method? Robert's use of sign language may depend on the education he has received, his environment, his family background (whether he grew up in an oral family or a culturally Deaf family) and/or at which point in his life he learned sign language. Language acquisition, regardless of the language, very much depends on exposure to language, structured learning and accidental learning opportunities. The interpreter that is provided will need to be aware of Robert's communication needs to ensure that he is fully aware of what concerns are being highlighted and is able to understand and translate these.

For example, if concerns of neglect are being raised, the social worker and interpreter need to make that clear and ensure that Robert has understood by gaining feedback to clarify. You may have noticed that in the case study of Robert he was described as Deaf, using a capital 'D'. This indicates that Robert is culturally Deaf, so his first language is most likely to be BSL; however, the method of sign language a person uses should never be assumed. While both BSL and SSE are visual languages using the hands to communicate, the structures of BSL and SSE are very different. BSL is a unique grammatical linguistic structure of sign language whereas SSE follows sign language in an English format and structure. If a person uses pure SSE, it is possible that BSL structure will not be fully comprehensible to them.

In the case of Robert, concerns around the issue of neglect are being raised. The Department of Health (1995) defines four categories of abuse: neglect, physical, sexual or emotional abuse (Children Act 1989). Whether concerns are around neglect, physical, emotional or sexual abuse, the concern needs to be clarified in the language that the parent understands. If this is not done, it could result in a parent with a sensory need not understanding the concerns or agreeing to something that they do not understand. The result of this could have disastrous consequences for the child and/or the parent.

A hearing parent(s) of a d/Deaf child

If a child is diagnosed as d/Deaf and the parent is hearing, the parent(s) may be unprepared and experience sadness, shock, guilt or bereavement and take time to adjust to the situation. Therefore working with parents requires sensitive, non-judgemental, empathic practice.

Lorraine Fletcher, a hearing mother whose second child was diagnosed as deaf at the age of ten months, wrote a book called *a Language for Ben. A Deaf child's right to sign* (1987). The impact of this book when understanding sensory issues from a parental perspective is both thought-provoking and moving. In the early part of the book, Lorraine Fletcher describes her feelings about Ben's diagnosis:

> *... And what of the cause? Maybe we could have been more aware even before Ben was born, more careful, perhaps? Yet during pregnancy, I was even more careful than during the last one: no alcohol, no drugs not even an aspirin.*

> (Fletcher, 1987, p24)

However, once Ben's family had adjusted to the initial feelings, Lorraine Fletcher continues:

> *Ben is still the same child, the child that Ray (Ben's dad) and I brought into the world in shared labour and the child we love ... No longer is it something ugly, a scar, a blemish. Faced with it, here and now, I see it as it has always been for Ben: a fact of life, and as it has to be for us: a difference.*

> (Fletcher, 1987, p25)

It could be argued that this poignant account relays how many hearing parents may feel when their child is first diagnosed as being deaf/Deaf. As the parents are hearing they may feel that the inability to hear is a loss, a disability. Theories of loss are discussed in more detail in Chapter 6. However, Fletcher argues that with appropriate support, in particular in the educational setting, a deaf/Deaf child can have opportunity and achieve, just the same as any other child. Therefore, it could be argued that sensory need is a difference that can be adjusted to if the child and/or parent(s) are given the appropriate support in relation to their specific sensory need.

Today, after much campaigning from RNID, BDA and other pro-d/Deaf organisations, parents and children are more aware of their rights. Ben was born in 1980 and it was considered that if a child did not learn to speak then they would be limited throughout their life. However, even today some parents do not have access to the same information as other parents, do not have the same understanding capacity or may be too shocked with the news that their child is deaf to move forward. Ben's parents were proactive in their quest for Ben to be able to be educated and communicate in the language for him, which was BSL.

However, not all parents will be as proactive, and in some families a child may use sign language at school, but at home family members will not be able to sign. Family members' inability to use a child's fundamental communication method can mean that a child may become isolated in his or her own home. This can lead not only to lack of family involvement, but lack of self-esteem and self-worth as the child sees other family members regularly interacting. As a practitioner, if you come across this situation, it would be important to encourage the family to sign in order to be able to communicate with their child.

It may be daunting for the parent because, as has previously been highlighted, sign language is another language and learning any new language is a challenge. However, as has also been highlighted, it can be learned at different levels and even a simple understanding of the child's language is most definitely better than no understanding. British Sign Language tuition can be sought at local colleges, or if the child attends a hearing-impaired unit or Deaf school, often the school will provide family sign language classes free of charge. Additionally, organisations that support and campaign on behalf of d/Deaf people also are a wealth of information. There may also be local groups in your area who provide family and one-to-one support. It is essential that you as a practitioner are proactive and creative in your practice to maximise the potential for each and every child that you work with, and especially those with a sensory need.

Deaf parent(s) of a Deaf child

Deaf people who use British Sign Language are seen as a linguistic minority (Campbell and Oliver, 2006). As culture, history, values, beliefs and Deaf identity are an integral part of Deafness, giving birth to a Deaf child would most likely be greeted with joy, not sadness. Deaf people marry each other 90 per cent of the time, and 10 per cent have Deaf children (Campbell and Oliver, 1996). Paddy Ladd was born Deaf in 1952 and was one of the first Deaf children to be placed into a hearing educational setting. Ladd highlights the plight of a Deaf child if oralism (oralists educate d/Deaf students using spoken language consisting of lip reading, speech, the process of watching mouth movements, and mastering breathing techniques) is the primary communicative method. In the book *Disability politics* (2006), Ladd considers the triumphs of Deaf educational settings *despite the disgusting work of oralists*. Ladd further highlights the importance of Deaf schools to enable Deaf children to socialise into the Deaf culture.

A Deaf child growing up in a Deaf family will acquire signing skills at a very early age. As they grow, their proficiency in signing skills grows also. This is why being taught in sign language is so important, as it is their first language. As children develop through the life stages, their learning is at its most advantageous when they learn in their first language. Imagine a child whose first language is BSL but every time they are in a classroom setting they have to learn through a third party. To illustrate, let us consider the case study of Giles.

CASE STUDY

Giles is 15 years old and in the process of taking his GCSEs. He is culturally Deaf and his first language is BSL. He attends a deaf unit in a mainstream school. As a result of a statement of educational need, he has been provided with a communication support worker (CSW) for every lesson. However, Giles does not get his tuition directly from the teacher as the hearing students do, as all the information has to be communicated via the CSW. While the CSW relays most of the information, realistically the information that is conveyed by the teacher to the other students at the time that the CSW is conveying the information to Giles is lost.

It could be argued that if Giles were to be educated in a school with small class groups, was taught directly in sign language by teachers qualified to a high BSL level (Levels 3/4) and in a culturally Deaf environment, his progress might then be comparable to that of students who are given the opportunity to learn directly from the teacher (for more information, see www.heathlands.herts.sch.uk/). It could further be argued that, unfortunately, this is not often the case, and due to the limited number of specialist schools, many d/Deaf children are educated in mainstream schools with deaf units. The key for us as workers is to maximise whatever resources are available and ensure that the children and families with which we work are aware of these resources.

Adapting use of language to individual requirement

As highlighted in the case studies used in this section, whichever language is being used, it needs to be adapted to individual requirements. To illustrate this point in relation to a child's sensory need, take the examples of Gustave and Ochi.

CASE STUDY

Gustave is hard of hearing, 8 years old and lives in the UK. Gustave wears digital hearing aids in both ears and has regular audiology appointments to ensure that the aids are providing the best transmission of sound. Gustave accesses a specialist unit for hearing-impaired children in a mainstream school. He has a statement of educational need which means that he has individual support throughout the schoolday, plus daily speech and language therapy. Gustave's mother is French and his father is English. Gustave's mother has ensured that her native tongue is integral to family life and therefore Gustave is bilingual. Gustave struggles a little with English comprehension, so has individual private lessons to improve his skills

---

CASE STUDY

Ochi is hard of hearing, 8 years old and lives in a village in Africa. He has school one hour per day. He has learned well, but could have learned so much more given a specialist environment, use of technological aids and opportunity. The remainder of his day, he is needed to cultivate the farm with his father and brothers to enable the family to be provided with food.

On average, children in the UK attend school for several hours per day and in general terms are not usually expected to work hard when they go home from school. If a health issue is identified then there is a health care system to address this. Additionally, if a learning need is highlighted, a child can be issued with a statement of educational need to enable them to have support (Education Act 1996, s.312/s.326).

ACTIVITY 5.2

Critically reflect on Ochi's learning and development opportunities. Do you think that Ochi would have the same language acquisition opportunities as Gustave?

Comment

Sensory-connected language acquisition is the same as any other language acquisition. People with sensory needs are educated in various ways depending on their opportunities.

When working with a parent or child who has a sensory requirement, ensure that their needs are individually met. Early preparation and getting to know the sensory needs of the children and parents with whom you work, may prove to be in the long term beneficial to the best interest of the child and thus well worth the extra effort it takes.

Every Child Matters

Following the report of the inquiry into the death of Victoria Climbié (Laming, 2003), the government responded with a Green Paper, *Every Child Matters.* This was adopted as the Children Act 2004, which provides the legal underpinning for Every Child Matters. The aim of the *Every Child Matters* initiative is to give every child the opportunity to achieve the five key outcomes:

- be healthy;
- stay safe;
- enjoy and achieve;
- make a positive contribution;
- achieve economic well-being (DoH, 2003).

(For more information, see www.dcsf.gov.uk/everychildmatters)

It could be argued that disabled children are one such group of children who do not fully enjoy the benefits of the Every Child Matters initiative. Four leading organisations, Contact a Family, Council for Disabled Children, Mencap and Special Educational Consortium, all of whom work with disabled children and their families, have joined forces to highlight and draw governmental attention to the fact that every child matters, disabled or non-disabled. Every Disabled Child Matters (EDCM) is a campaign to get rights and justice for every disabled child. Campaigners argue this action has been necessary because disabled children, young people and their families have been left out for too long and EDCM is the campaign to correct this. The aim of the campaign is for all disabled children and their families to have the right to the services and support they need to live ordinary lives. (For more information, see www.edcm.org.uk) It is essential for a child with a sensory need to have equity as it could be argued that inequalities such as these can contribute to vulnerability for such children.

Munro (1999) outlined common errors of reasoning in child protection work, which included:

- workers with limited knowledge;
- errors in human reasoning, which can be avoided if workers are aware of them and endeavour to address them;
- inaccurate records – this could be avoided by analytical practice, e.g. check lists and not overlooking the *dull, abstract, statistical and old* (p22);
- lack of preparation to change your mind if you uncover further evidence.

It could be argued that Munro makes an excellent point when highlighting that *profes-sionals' judgements should be regarded as valuable but fallible, needing to be treated as hypotheses requiring further testing* (Munro, 1999, p22). This is even more so in a sensory context as lack of sensory knowledge or communicative skills may cloud initial percep-tions. If a practitioner becomes aware that the situation was not as they first perceived, specialist sensory support should be sought.

Child deaths continue to occur, most recently in case of Baby Peter, which further high-lights the need for risk assessment and management. Whether there is a sensory need or not, there is a constant need for social workers and indeed all professionals to use chro-nologies, use analytical tools, be vigilant with accurate record keeping, keep up to date with current research/knowledge, practice policy, guidance and legislation.

Assessment frameworks

In 2000, The Department of Health provided guidance for assessment in the form of the *Framework for the Assessment of Children in Need and their Families* (in this section this will be referred to as the assessment framework). See Figure 5.1.

Figure 5.1 The assessment triangle

(*Source:* Department of Health, 2000)

The government identified that in order to improve the lives of vulnerable and disadvan-taged groups of children, an understanding of what was actually happening in their lives needed to be realised in order for appropriate action to take place. To collate the appropri-ate information to enable this framework to benefit children, an extensive consultation took place with research about the needs of children from a multi-agency perspective. Further, to ensure a comprehensive way of working the assessment framework was also incorporated into the *Working together to safeguard children* (Department of Health et al., 2006).

ACTIVITY 5.3

Looking at the diagram of the assessment framework. Who do you think will use it? Which legislation do you think influenced it? What do you think the purpose of the assessment framework is? What do you think is hoped to be achieved by this type of assessment?

Comment

The assessment framework was primarily introduced for professionals and other staff involved in carrying out assessments for children in need and their families under s.17 of the Children Act 1989. The Framework for Assessment document (Department of Health, 2000) is issued under s.7 of the Local Authority Social Services Act 1970, which requires local authorities to act under the guidance of the Secretary of State. Social services have the lead responsibility for assessment of children in need and also those at risk of significant harm under s.47 of the Children Act 1989. Other professionals have a responsibility to assist social services in the collation of the information required for the assessment framework. The main emphasis in social work should be to provide services to support children to remain with their families unless risk factors override this. You may have critically reflected on the purpose of the assessment framework as being an analytical tool to systematically understand and record what is actually happening in the life of the child.

When assessing a child with a sensory need, your assessment may need additional vigilance. Information collated needs to be accurate, therefore accurate information gathering needs to be undertaken. This can only be done if appropriate communicative methods are used when working with children and families with a sensory need. There are various methods for collating information and we will explore some of these next.

ACTIVITY 5.4

What other assessment tools can you think of?

Comment

You may have thought of genograms or ecomaps.

Genogram

A genogram enables you to visually map a family tree and can prove to be very useful when working with complex family structures. Symbols can be added to a genogram to enable a clearer picture to develop. In current genograms, certain symbols are already used, as shown in Figure 5.2.

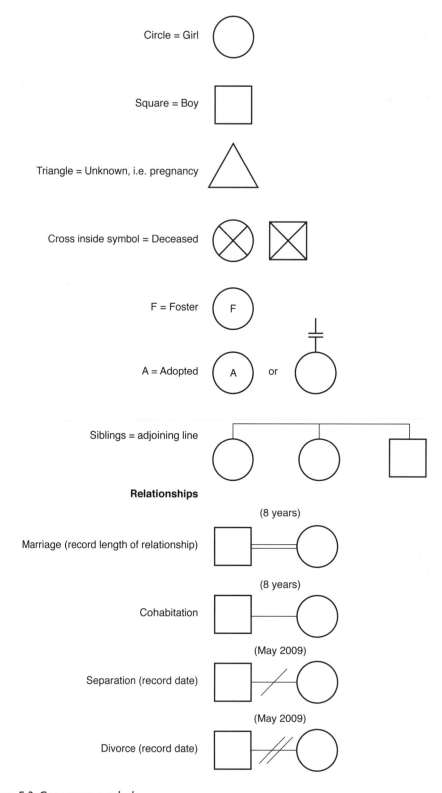

Figure 5.2 Genogram symbols

A genogram can be adapted to the specific client group with which you work. For the purpose of this genogram we will also use bold letters to identify a child's sensory and/or communicative need.

- deaf/Deaf (**d,D**) As highlighted in previous chapters, if a person is culturally '**D**' Deaf it is essential to have an understanding of this, to ensure good practice and appropriate intervention, i.e. sign language interpreter. If the person is '**d**' it is also vital to ascertain the preferred method of communication, i.e. lipspeaking, BSL, SSE and so on.

- Deafblind (**DB**).

- Visually impaired (**VI**).

- Verbal (**V**).

- Non-verbal (**NV**).

- British Sign Language (**BSL**).

- Sign Supported English (**SSE**).

- Makaton (**M**).

- Hands-on signing (**HOS**).

- Deafblind Manual (**DBM**).

To illustrate use of a genogram combined with sensory abbreviations, we will use the case study of Annabelle.

CASE STUDY

Annabelle is 6 years old and attends a specialist school for children who are visually impaired. She has been referred to the duty team following a referral from her school. Annabelle has been arriving at school in dirty clothes and she repeatedly has untreated headlice episodes.

As highlighted earlier, a circle indicates a girl, i.e. Annabelle. Next, add date of birth, sensory need and communication method, as in Figure 5.3.

Figure 5.3 Annabelle

At a glance you can now tell that Annabelle is 6 years old, is visually impaired, uses verbal communication and hands-on signing. Verbal communication is noted first, as this is her preferred method of communication.

ACTIVITY 5.5

You have been asked to visit Annabelle and her family and gather information to enable you to intervene appropriately. You have been made aware by the referrer that Annabelle comes from a large family with complex circumstances. Annabelle's birth parents are divorced. Mum is deaf (note the small 'd') and uses verbal communication/BSL and hands-on signing HOS). Dad is profoundly Deaf (culturally 'D' Deaf) and uses BSL/HOS. Mum's new partner is also profoundly Deaf, with BSL as his first language. Dad's new wife is profoundly Deaf with the first language of BSL. Annabelle's eldest brother is Deaf and his first language is BSL; he also uses HOS to communicate with Annabelle. Annabelle's other siblings are hearing but all communicate in verbal, BSL and hands-on signing.

Use a genogram to map out Annabelle's complex family tree.

Your genogram may look like the one shown in Figure 5.4.

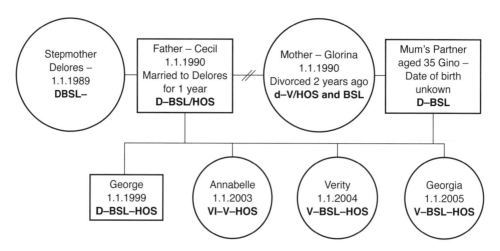

Figure 5.4 Annabelle's genogram

It is good practice to indicate the sensory need first, followed by the preferred method of communication and then subsequent methods of communication, for example George **D–BSL–HOS** indicates that George is culturally Deaf, his first language is British Sign Language, however, he also communicates using hands-on signing.

It is good to practise using genograms prior to use in practice. This enables the worker to have a clear understanding of symbols/letters they wish to use. It also ensures that genogram compilation does not provoke any values or feelings within the worker that need to be addressed prior to working with the child. For example, a worker may have recently experienced the death of a family member and working through the genogram with the family may evoke a range of feelings.

Ecomaps

An ecomap explores the support networks a child has within its environment. This can take into account the nuclear family, extended family, friendships, pets, organisations, clubs, religion, culture, other professionals (e.g. school) and the wider community. The ecomap shows the different ways that various people interact with the child at different levels on a daily basis, and the effect this has on the child. Ecomaps are an ongoing assessment tool as the child's situation may change, therefore a number of ecomaps may be necessary for each child with whom you work. Ecomaps can be used in diagram form as illustrated in Figure 5.5.

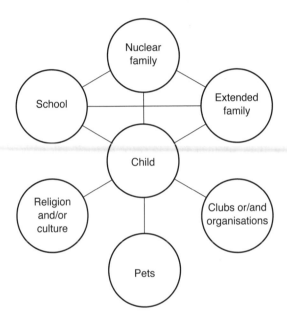

Figure 5.5 Ecomap

As highlighted in the ecomap in Figure 5.5 information collation can highlight if for example the extended family have contact with the nuclear family, or if the school have contact with the parent(s)/carers/extended family. The ecomap can be as simple or complex as the child's situation necessitates. You as the worker can keep the ecomap simple if that is what enables you to understand the child's individual needs. However, it is important to bear in mind that the deeper your exploration, the more information and the bigger the picture you will accumulate in regard to the child's needs.

When working with children an optional way to explore ecomaps is to use play. To illustrate we will look at the case study of Luean.

> **CASE STUDY**
>
> *Luean is 6 years old. He has been referred to your team because there are investigations into sexual abuse allegations involving Luean within his family. Luean is sight and hearing impaired, but with the use of glasses and hearing aids in both ears he communicates verbally. Luean has not been very communicative in the time you have been working with him. You have tried various direct work options such as encouraging Luean to draw his feelings using story books/paint/paper/other craft materials, but none has worked. You decide to try using the ecomap system. You have decided to use play people (maybe such as you would use in a doll's house). You have drawn up an emotions board with lots of different faces, some happy some sad, some frightened. You have asked Luean to choose a play person that represents him and other family members. You asked Luean if he would like to choose a play person to represent you as the worker, but he has declined this. Luean can then choose which face he would like to place which play person on. This process may identify how Luean is thinking and feeling and enable you to provide appropriate support and intervention that he needs.*

Another ecomap option is to use buttons of all different shapes and sizes. Buttons are a good method because they are small, light to carry, tactile (particularly good for a child with a sensory need) and you can always have them with you. You could ask the child to identify which button would they choose to be themselves and which buttons they would choose for other people they come into contact with. You could again use the emotions board or just construct play with the buttons, literally to make it child-orientated play. When working with a child with a sensory need, it is may be necessary to ensure you have buttons with different tactile surfaces, so that the child does not identify just by sight but also by touch. This process can show you who is involved with the child and in which capacity.

Attachment theory

As you are progressing through your degree course, you are likely to become aware of attachment theory and the works of John Bowlby (1969, 1973, 1988). Attachment theory can be seen as *a theory of personality development in the context of close relationships* (Howe, 2001, p194). Attachment theory argues that children begin to develop mental representations of their own worth in the form of *internal working models*, which are based upon the availability of other people and their ability and willingness to provide care (Ainsworth et al., 1978; Howe, 2001, p200).

Bowlby drew on early developments in the study of animal behaviour (ethology) and was influenced by one of the earlier known theorists, Konrad Lorenz. Lorenz was known among bologists for his work on imprinting on young animals. Lorenz found that animals learned very young in their lives who their caregivers would be. Lorenz found that by substituting himself as the caregiver to animals in their infancy, they would imprint on him. This became famous as the experiment of imprinting among young geese, where he induced geese to think he was their mother. Lorenz drew upon his experience of animal research to analyse human behaviour. However, Lorenz's work became contentious because he theorised that behavioural tendencies are instinctive and not able to be modified by later experiences.

Bowlby supported this theory as he theorised that infants had a biological need or an instinct to form an attachment with the caregiver, traditionally perceived as the mother (Crawford and Walker, 2007). Bowlby's early work on maternal deprivation concluded that prolonged separation, especially in the first five years of a child's life, between mother and child could result in delinquency or mental health issues. Bowlby theorised that if the child did not have its mother's love in the early years, this would have an impact on the child's emotional development which could have long-lasting effects.

In a sensory context, children are sometimes hospitalised for long periods of time in their early years due to complex medical needs. While a child with a sensory need may be part of a loving family environment, their sensory needs may not have been identified due to the level of complex medical needs and thus formal communication not established. This may result in a mother not communicating with her child in a conventional way. However, it could be argued that even where there are long periods of separation in the early years, attachment with a child can be built by trusting emotional response and body language provided by the caregiver.

Resilience

Resilience is defined as *normal development under difficult conditions* (Fonagy et al., 1994, p231). Resilience in children explores why some children are more susceptible and are deeply affected by their experiences and other children may resist the difficulties they experience and recover more quickly from their traumatic experiences.

Horwarth (2004) discusses how a child's day-to-day functioning is affected by the balance between harmful and protective factors throughout their lives. Therefore, it is very important to look for the positive factors that the child experiences in their lives to maximise the child's potential to achieve resilience (Kirby and Fraser, 1997).

An important protective factor is that the child has a significant adult who will provide support during difficult times, which can include a professional worker (Jenkins and Smith, 1990). If a child has a sensory need, it is essential that the significant adult be sensory aware. The worker need not be experienced initially, as their expertise may be in the area of substance misuse or domestic violence, but when beginning work with the child, the worker could contact specialist organisations to get guidance on working with a child with a sensory need. For example, SENSE produces information for working with deaf-blind children. While this would need to be adapted to the child's specific need, there is information that will relate to communication tactics, which are essential for working with children at their specific communicative level in order to address their specific need. When working with children it is important to consider the factors which influence resilience.

Factors which promote resilience

- Higher IQ.

- Good attachment /trusting relationships/good relationships with siblings.

- Individual communication (BSL, clear speech, deafblind manual).

- Awareness of and understanding of need (e.g. sensory awareness).

- Positive role models/support network (school, wider family, community, religion, culture, etc.).

- Encouraging autonomy, choice, independence and well-being to promote self-esteem.

Factors which influence vulnerability

- Disability – a child can become more susceptible with each additional disability, e.g. deafblindness (complexity of dual sensory loss).

- Age.

- Poverty.

- Domestic violence, substance misuse, mental health issues.

- Abusive past, especially in early childhood.

- Environment.

- Poor support network, family, school, friends – social isolation.

Being alert to sensory support needed by a child can contribute to resilience. The worker does not have to be an expert, but rather to have a willingness to get to know the child and their sensory need. The support you provide is likely to contribute to that child's independence, well-being and choice and support them to achieve.

Legislation

Regardless of the practice area of children and families social work that you choose to work in, the same legislation, guidance, policies and procedures will apply. The Children Act 1989 underpins all social work practice in this complex area of social work. However, while the work can be complex and demanding, it can also be rewarding.

Other legislation you will find that you work with the most when working with a child with a sensory need and possibly other additional needs are the Education Act 1996 and Special Educational Needs and Disability Act 2001.

The Children Act 1989 specifically facilitates support for children in need, children at risk of significant harm, their families and carers. The 2004 amendment has greater focus on safeguarding issues. The Education Act 1996 (s.7) highlights that school attendance is not compulsory, parents can choose to educate at home or otherwise. A parent with a child who has sensory needs or other disabilities may choose to educate their child at home; however, they must satisfy the local education authority that the education being provided to the child is satisfactory. When a child attends school, regular attendance is compulsory and if a child truants the parents can be prosecuted or the child can be placed on an Education Supervision Order (s.36, Children Act 1989).

Diversity and equality are addressed by the provision made in the Education Act 2002 which gives parents the rights to withdraw their children from specifically religious-focused assemblies. If a child has a disability which facilitates the need for them to attend a school outside of mainstream education, the child is entitled to an assessment to determine the level of need required (s.312, Children Act 1996). If a statement of educational need is issued then the education authority has a duty to meet the needs of the child to enable him/her to be educationally supported. If a statement application is refused, parents have a right to appeal to the Special Educational Needs and Disability Tribunal (s.326, Education Act 1996; Johns, 2009). As was highlighted earlier in the case of Ben, when a child has a sensory need, it is essential that their specific needs are met to enable them to aspire to their full potential.

While the legislative framework is in place and the final decision is an educational one, often parents find the process very stressful and social work support can prove to be invaluable.

Culture, race and diversity

Bernard's (1999) research investigated problems experienced by black children with learning disabilities who had been sexually abused. Bernard's study highlighted that black disabled children had to deal with multiple layers of racism and oppression in a predominantly Eurocentric society in addition to the oppression and discrimination experienced as a disabled child. While Bernard's research was with children with learning disabilities, it could be argued that children with sensory needs are equally vulnerable.

Within an increasingly global society, it is essential that workers ensure their practice is anti-discriminatory and sensory aware. If as workers we are working with a service user with a sensory need or from a culture or race that we have not worked with before, we need to develop our understanding. The action of showing respect accompanied by a basic level of understanding may enable you to work more effectively with a family and really understand where they are coming from. If you understand the issues involved for the children you work with it will enable you to tailor-make your intervention.

Additionally, by being culturally aware you may avoid making assumptions and stereotyping and avoid making wrong judgements. Cultural awareness may enable you to challenge cultural practices that are not in the best interest of the child or that constitute abuse in the UK.

Thus, responding to multicultural, multi-ethnic and multi-faith challenges can be addressed by advance preparation and understanding individual need. This challenge is not always easy and could be described as complex and dynamic (Owusu-Bempah, 2000) because we all have our own value bases. Furthermore, in order to meet needs, we need to be knowledgeable, informed and empathic (Cree and Macaulay, 2001). An understanding of the diversity of each and every child you work with is essential if practice is to be effective, individual and flexible to each child's needs. This holds greater significance for each child as they move through the stages of life, and in particular if sensory needs are combined with cultural needs.

A culturegram (see Figure 5.6) can be used as an assessment tool to help a worker understand cultural diversity. A culturegram could focus on:

- legal status;
- age at which child entered UK;
- first language;
- English as a second language;
- reason for relocation;
- time spent in UK/current community;
- religious beliefs;
- contact/support, e.g. religious, cultural, community or other;
- special events either personal or linked with culture;
- crisis/traumatic experiences;
- family values, hierarchy and dynamics;
- education;
- employment;
- additional values or beliefs.

By using a culturegram as an assessment tool you may find your approach is more sensitive while still being thorough. Furthermore, you could also use the same sensory abbreviators as used in the genogram to highlight a child's sensory needs. As a social worker you may be asked to assess a situation of which you have no prior knowledge and you may feel this is a daunting prospect. However, using a culturegram as a framework can have a positive impact on the information you collate.

The collation of information enables the social worker to practise from a person-centred perspective and provide individual intervention. It could be argued that children with complex needs are more prone to vulnerability and thus individual intervention is imperative.

The Department for Children, Schools and Families has recognised the vulnerability of disabled children to abuse and has issued specific guidance (DCSF, 2009). Where there are cases of abuse, it is important to recognise that a black disabled child may not only have to face a child protection service as a disabled child but there may not be the cultural sensitivity that is required for their needs (Bernard, 1999). Bernard (1999) highlighted that *disabled children with additional needs are known to be more vulnerable to abuse* (Bernard, 1999, p327) and yet disabled children are less likely to be represented in the child protection investigations (Morris, 1995).

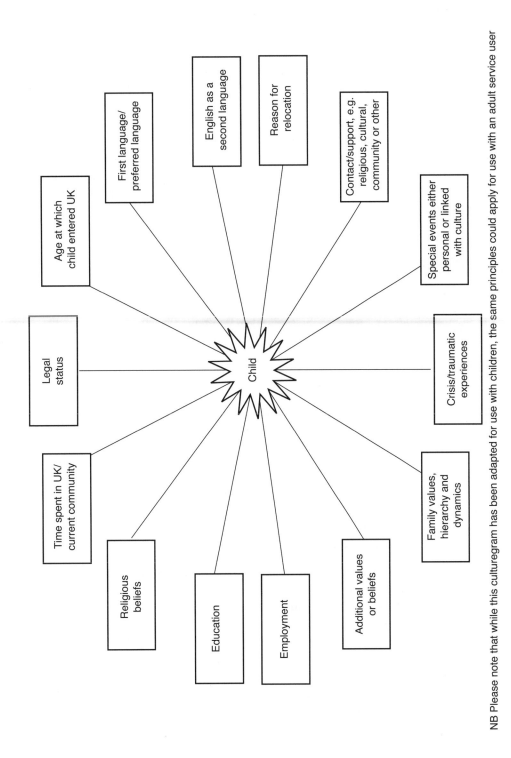

Figure 5.6 Culturegram

> ### CASE STUDY
>
> *Waitimu is 7 years old and has cerebral palsy, associated learning difficulties and is reg-*
> *istered blind. Waitimu's mother came from Africa to the UK when Waitimu was 4 years*
> *old. As a disabled children's service social worker you are working with Waitimu and his*
> *mother. Waitimu communicates using limited speech. You communicate effectively with*
> *Waitimu as you have got to know his individual communication needs. Upon one of your*
> *visits Waitimu's mother tells you she has begun a new relationship. However, a couple*
> *of visits later, Waitimu tells you that Mum's new friend does not like him. Upon inves-*
> *tigation, Waitimu tells you that the new friend hits him very hard if he makes a noise.*
> *Waitimu shows you large bruises on the top of his leg and says that Mum's friend did*
> *them. When you approach Mum she says that 'chastisement' is very important in her cul-*
> *ture and if Waitimu is naughty, he will be punished.*

> ### ACTIVITY 5.6
>
> *Think about the research highlighted by Bernard (1999) and Morris (1995). How do you*
> *think you would approach this sensitive situation? Remember that you must avoid asking*
> *any leading questions as it may hinder any child protection investigation under s.47 of the*
> *Children Act 1989 that may be necessary, and remember the importance of reporting the*
> *incident to the senior in your team.*

Comment

In this case Waitimu disclosed the abuse. However, Bernard's (1999) research further revealed that often abuse is not reported. The reasons could be fear of stigma, children unable to communicate abuse; professionals unable to detect abuse, and lack of corroboratory evidence and thus difficulties in proving abuse. Cross (1998) argues that there are some who 'like' to believe that disabled children are not affected by their experiences because they do not understand what is happening to them but Bernard (1999) argues that even when a child communicates abuse has taken place often disabled children are not viewed as *credible witnesses* (p326).

As Bernard's study highlighted earlier, black disabled children not only have disability to contend with but oppression, discrimination and in some cases abuse. A clear use of a culturegram as an assessment tool could be useful in understanding the child's experiences and detecting abuse. It is not only a useful approach to issues of culture difference with sensitivity but it can also be sensitively used in the case of allegations of abuse. Any allegations need to be taken seriously, further investigations made in a multi-agency environment and a decision made. These decisions are not made in isolation, but rather in collaboration and partnership with local authority managers and other agencies to enable the best outcome for the child.

However, whatever intervention we implement it is essential to remember that the welfare of the child is paramount in deciding all questions about his or her upbringing (s.1.1, Children Act 1989). A worker must also take into account the principle that regard is taken into account what the implications will be for that child if there is a delay in decision (s.1.1, Children Act 1989). Furthermore, any worker working with children, whether they are disabled, non-disabled, have a sensory need or do not, must always consider the wishes and feelings of the child, taking into account age and understanding (s.1.15, Children Act 1989).

General Social Care Council (GSCC) and Children's Workforce Development Council (CWDC)

As a student on the degree programme and soon to become a qualified social worker, registration with the General Social Care Council (GSCC) will be fundamental. If you choose to work in a child and family setting it is also essential that not only are you registered but also that you have an understanding of how the Children's Workforce Development Council (CWDC) works.

GSCC

The GSCC was established in October 2001 under the Care Standards Act 2000 and sponsored by the Department of Health, while also working closely with the Department for Children, Schools and Families in delivering the children's and young people's care agenda. The GSCC is responsible for codes of practice, which have no doubt been integral in your current training, the Social Care Register and social work education and training. The codes of practice will continue to be an integral part of your practice upon qualification, as service users and carers can check the registration of a social worker and establish whether they meet the GSCC standards, and they can raise concerns about the conduct of a registered social worker and ask the GSCC to investigate. The Social Care Register currently consists of student and qualified social workers (UK and international). However, in the future the GSCC aims to open the register to other groups of care workers. All qualified social workers should be registered and you may find that a requirement for application to a social work post is that you are GSCC registered. It is interesting to note that the title 'social worker' has been protected by law in England since 1 April 2005 as this law came from the Care Standards Act 2000 to ensure that only those who are properly qualified, registered and accountable for their work describe themselves as social workers (GSCC, 2001).

Children's Workforce Development Council (CWDC)

CWDC supports over half a million people in the children's workforce across England, including those in child care provision, learning mentors, education welfare, foster care and social care (CWDC, 2009). It was set up in 2005 to support the implementation of Every Child Matters, a new approach to the well-being of children and young people from birth to age 19. Through the Every Child Matters programme, the government's aim is for every child to have the support they need to achieve the five key outcomes, which we discussed earlier in the chapter.

The CWDC aims to improve the lives of children, young people, their families and carers by ensuring that those who work with children and young people have the best possible training, qualifications and support. It is one of six bodies forming the UK Skills For Care and Development Sector Skills Council and co-ordinates the Children's Workforce Network. The Skills for Care and Development Sector Skills Council is an alliance of six organisations. These are:

- Care Council for Wales;
- Children's Workforce Development Council;
- General Social Care Council;
- Northern Ireland Social Care Council;
- Scottish Social Services Council;
- Skills for Care.

The CWDC has two roles: Sector Skills Council (SSC) body and workforce reform agency. There are 25 Sector Skills Councils for the UK workforce. Together they form the Skills for Business Network (SfBN). Each SSC works to agree priorities and targets with its employers and partners to address the four key goals:

- reducing skills gaps and shortages;
- improving productivity, business and public service performance;
- increasing opportunities to boost the skills and productivity of everyone in the sector's workforce, including action on equal opportunities;
- improving learning supply, including apprenticeships, higher education and national occupational standards.

The Children's Workforce Network (CWN) is an alliance of 12 partners, one of which is CWDC, all committed to creating and supporting a world-class children's workforce in England. CWN is a strategic body, bringing together the relevant Sector Skills Councils and other partners representing the workforce. It is a voluntary grouping of independent partners, who recognise that collaboration will help them to achieve the more effective implementation of their individual and joint roles (CWDC, 2009).

Another aspect of support provided by the CWDC is to newly qualified social workers (NQSWs). Over three years from September 2008, CWDC is working with employers to pilot a comprehensive programme of support for NQSWs that offers:

- a comprehensive induction schedule through their first year of employment;
- high-quality supervision and training;
- easy-to-use guidance materials;
- a professional development plan designed to increase confidence and maximise capability.

In its first year, the programme supported 1,000 NQSWs working for 89 employers. Participation is open to people who have recently qualified as a social worker or who have completed less than six months' work as a qualified social worker. The support package has been designed to ensure that NQSWs receive consistent, high-quality support and that those supervising NQSWs are confident in their skills to provide support. The aim of the programme is to contribute to increasing the number of people who continue their long-term career within social work with children and families.

While the CWDC continues with the NQSW programme they have also introduced an Early Professional Development Pilot programme for years 2 and 3 of a social work career. The purpose of the programme is to:

- improve recruitment and retain children's social workers;
- improve training and development opportunities for social workers;
- improve social work practice;
- promote and improve effective supervision.

Social workers on this programme have six outcome statements to achieve. These cover:

- information gathering;
- analysing information and making recommendations;
- planning, implementation and review;
- working directly with children, young people, their families and carers;
- safeguarding, child protection and promoting the welfare of children and young people;
- professional development.

The purpose of working towards covering these outcome statements is to use them as a developmental framework to improve the quality of practice and improve service provision to children, families and their carers (for more information see **www.cwdc.co.uk**).

For more information on being a newly qualified worker see Keen et al. (2009) *Newly qualified social workers: A handbook for practice*.

C H A P T E R   S U M M A R Y

This chapter has introduced you to the key issues in a children and families setting and identified how sensory awareness is important to effective intervention. These have been explored from both the child's and the parents' perspectives and you have been introduced to practical assessment tools, such as genograms, ecomaps and culturegrams. The theoretical frameworks of resilience and attachment theory have been discussed and applied to case study material. The principal legislation and policies have been identified and the roles of key organisations have been outlined.

Department of Health (2000) *Framework for the assessment of children in need and their families.* London: The Stationery Office.

This guidance draws widely on a wealth of research about the needs of children and the best practice. A key component of the government's objectives for children's social services is the development of a framework for assessing children in need and their families, to ensure a timely response and effective provision of services. See page 89 of this guidance for the Assessment Framework. The Assessment Framework has been incorporated into *Working Together to Safeguard Children* (Department of Health et al., 2006).

Jowitt, M and O'Loughlin, S (2007) *Social work with children and families.* Exeter: Learning Matters.

Social work with children and families is one of the most challenging and rewarding areas of social work practice. Social workers can make a significant difference to the life of a child by providing protection and preventing them from suffering from significant harm. This book provides an overview of the principal elements of social work with children and families, outlining the knowledge social workers need to ensure the protection of children, and the skills which enable social workers to work effectively with children and families.

White, R, Carr, P and Lowe, N (2002) *The Children Act in practice.* Third edition. London: LexisNexis Butterworths.

The Children Act 1989, which came into force in October 1991, introduced a radical reform of court procedure. At the same time the government published extensive guidance for practitioners on how the new provisions would have effect. In the years that followed, a wealth of decisions has provided authoritative interpretation of the statutory provisions but has also raised important new issues. The third edition of the best-selling guide to the Children Act 1989 has been completely rewritten to take account of all relevant legislative and case law developments, relating to the most important and far-reaching reform of child law in the twentieth century.

Horner, N and Krawczyk, S (2006) *Social work in education and children's services.* Exeter: Learning Matters.

The Children Act 2004 made it clear that the education sector is at the centre of government plans to address the universal needs and well-being of children and young people. This book addresses these profound changes in the child welfare landscape and gives practitioners working with children, young people and their families a clear explanation of the current and anticipated inter-relationship between social work and education. This book concentrates on the small but very significant number of children and young people for whom schooling is potentially or actually difficult. Such children and young people are most likely to be involved in the specialist or targeted services staffed by various professionals, including social workers.

Stanley, N and Manthorpe, J (eds) (2004) *The age of inquiry: Learning and blaming in health and social care.* London: Routledge.

This book examines inquiries across a range of services: into child protection tragedies, mental health homicides, abuse in learning disability services and in residential nursing care for older people. The contributors to this book discuss a wide range of inquiries in terms of processes, findings and applications. Readers will find new and original accounts of high-profile inquiries such as the Climbié inquiry, as well as being introduced to inquiries that are less familiar.

Chapter 6
Mental health and sensory needs

Introduction

The Office of National Statistics (2000) states that mental health problems affect one in six adults at any one time. This refers to 'significant' mental health problems and other studies state that mental health problems are more frequent (Goldberg and Huxley, 1992).

Consequently, it is likely that you will work with people experiencing mental health problems in whatever area of social work that you work in after qualifying. Consequently, mental health is a key area for you to gain knowledge, understanding and skills of your future practice. Golightley (2008) highlights the importance of students in social work education gaining a thorough understanding of this key area and the impact this will have on their social work practice.

While this chapter will allow the student to have an overview of mental health issues, the primary focus will be in relation to mental health and sensory need. In this chapter, you will be introduced to key terminology used and see how some of the theoretical models have influenced the language used. We will revisit the distinction between the medical and social models that you were first introduced to in Chapter 3, as these models are central to understanding the key controversies in mental health. The major forms of mental health problems will be outlined and applied to the case studies, which we will be following throughout the chapter.

A range of social models will be outlined and discrimination relating to race and ethnicity, gender and sexual orientation will be discussed. Specific issues for people with sensory needs will be explored and recent policy developments to address inequalities in access for deaf people with mental health needs will be outlined. But first of all, let us meet two people that we will be following through the chapter:

CASE STUDY

Ronnie is a 19-year-old, black African Caribbean man who was born deaf to hearing parents. As he grew up, he learnt British Sign Language, became interested in the Deaf community and has developed a positive identity as a Deaf person. Ronnie is currently studying at university on the first year of a degree course. Although his studies went well at first, things have deteriorated recently. He has stopped going to lectures and spends increasing amounts of time at home in his room. His friends have noticed that, when they occasionally do see him, his behaviour seems erratic and he has become preoccupied with fixed views about minor things. They are worried and think that Ronnie is 'not himself'.

Valerie is a 72-year-old white British woman. Six months ago, her husband died after an extended illness and she lives alone in a rural community. Valerie's eyesight has been deteriorating for some time and she no longer feels safe to drive, which severely restricts her ability to get out. Her son lives nearby and tries to visit as often as he can but he has his own family. He has noticed that his mother seems low in mood and she and her home look increasingly unkempt. She does not show her usual pleasure in cooking, saying that 'she can't be bothered'.

We will be following Ronnie and Valerie throughout the chapter. To review any issues relating to sensory need, see Chapter 1. In the next section, we will explore what we mean by mental health problems.

What are mental health problems?

Mental health is a highly contested area that has always been characterised by conflicting perspectives. It has also always featured highly stigmatised language.

ACTIVITY 6.1

1. *Think back to your childhood and the first messages you received about mental ill health. Jot down the words and phrases used to describe people with mental health problems.*

2. *Take note of the feelings you associate with these messages.*

Comment

You may have found that you have received rather negative messages about mental health problems. It is quite common for people with mental health problems to be stigmatised and seen as 'different' (Green et al., 2003). There are a considerable number of negative terms that are used to describe people who experience mental health problems.

Terminology and key definitions

As well as negative, stigmatising language, the highly contested nature of mental health is reflected in the different terminology used by different theoretical perspectives. Within the medical model, the term 'mental illness' is most commonly used. Within social models, terms such as 'mental distress' have been historically favoured because they do not medicalise human experience and separate people off from the 'normal' population. The term 'mental health problem' has been used in this book because it represents a relatively neutral middle ground that does not subscribe to a particular theoretical position.

The medical and social models revisited

In Chapter 3, you were introduced to the distinction between the medical and social models of disability and in particular in relation to sensory need. We discussed how the medical model is inclined to centre on either the biological or psychological aspects of disability, whereas the social model is inclined to focus on structural or cultural aspects of disability (Priestley, 2003). In Chapter 3, we highlighted how a small piece of intervention for someone who has a sensory need can remove societal barriers such as in the case study of William, whose barrier was his deterioration in eyesight and the way in which this was overcome by the provision of prescriptive glasses. However, where there are mental health needs combined with sensory needs the individual then experiences greater complexity of need. The tendancy of the medical model being inclined to focus on biological and physical aspects of disability is particularly true in the field of mental health and these theoretical positions are central to understanding the key controversies in mental health.

The medical model focuses on the process of diagnosis and treatment in a similar process to physical disease. It provides a framework for understanding the main forms of mental health problems that we shall discuss in this chapter.

The social model refers to a range of different approaches that place a strong emphasis on the social aspects of mental health. These include an emphasis on life events to approaches such as labelling theory that challenge the traditional medical process of diagnosis and treatment. We shall return to these later in the chapter.

User involvement in mental health

There is a long history of user groups and user involvement in mental health, starting in the US in the 1960s and the Netherlands in the 1970s (Wallcraft and Nettle, 2009). Key texts, such as Judi Chamberlain's *On our own,* helped develop a critique of the ways in which mental health services worked. The British user movement developed in the 1980s and represents a wide spectrum of opinions. Some user-led organisations such as the UK Advocacy Network were relatively mainstream, while groups such as Survivors Speak Out formed a radical critique of mental health services. For example, an early user movement leader, Eric Irwin, famously stated that people with mental health problems are 'consumers' of mental health services in the same way that woodlice are consumers of Rentokil! (Wallcraft and Nettle, 2009, p8). The British Society for Mental Health and Deafness highlights that where mental health needs are combined with sensory needs, appropriate policies are required to enable development of accessible mental health services for deaf people. An example of this would be that a person whose first language is BSL would have access to a qualified sign language interpreter at mental health appointments to ensure that all information was conveyed in the Deaf person's first language.

The main forms of mental health problems

The two widely established systems used to classify mental disorders are the International Classification of Disease (ICD 10) developed by the World Health Organisation and the Diagnostic and Statistical Manual of Mental Disorders (DSM IV-TR) used in the US. These provide standard criteria to guide diagnosis and have deliberately tried to converge their codes in recent revisions. Since the nature of mental health problems varies considerably, it will be useful for us to look at the main forms of mental health problems that people experience.

Schizophrenia and other psychotic disorders

Schizophrenia is a form of psychotic disorder that has been an historically important diagnosis and one that has provoked considerable controversy. Schizophrenia is commonly thought to mean 'split personality' and psychosis is often linked with dangerousness but both of these are misconceptions. Schizophrenia affects key mental processes that affect our sense of self and is traditionally divided into positive and negative symptoms. Positive symptoms include hallucinations (experiencing things that others cannot experience) and delusions (beliefs that others find implausible). Negative symptoms include a sense of apathy, difficulties in concentration and wanting to avoid others.

If I was experiencing psychosis, my ability to distinguish between what is real and what is unreal would be seriously affected. I may hear people saying things when no one is speaking (known as auditory hallucinations) or believe that other people can hear my thoughts (thought broadcasting). I may develop strong persistent beliefs (delusions) which are unbelievable to others around me who know me well, such as a belief that TV presenters are speaking to me personally (ideas of reference). These experiences are likely to leave me feeling bewildered, frightened and suspicious of other people who do not share my perceptions or beliefs. There are a number of similar conditions, such as schizoaffective and schizophreniform disorders that share many but not all of the features of schizophrenia.

CASE STUDY

Ronnie has been in his room for almost a week. The last time that he went to his lecture, he had a frightening experience on the way home. He was travelling home by bus and felt that other passengers were controlling his thoughts. He stopped watching television because last night, he was watching the news and he felt that the news reader was talking to him personally through coded messages and was controlling his thoughts and feelings. He felt quite overwhelmed by these experiences and decided to stay in his room for a few days to 'get his head straight' because he could no longer tell what was inside his head and what was outside.

Comment

Ronnie could be seen as experiencing a number of the symptoms of a psychotic condition, such as schizophrenia. His feeling that others can control his thoughts is an example of thought insertion. His experience of feeling that the news reader was speaking to him personally is an example of having ideas of reference. These experiences alone can be quite frightening and bewildering. However, critically reflect on Ronnie as a Deaf person with mental health issues. Not only would he have these frightening experiences to deal with but he may not be able to access information in his first language, nor have access to a human aid to communication who can communicate with him at a time when he really needs it. In Chapter 2, a wide range of communication methods was outlined and it might be helpful to remind yourself of the communication methods that would be available. Organisations such as the British Society for Mental Health and Deafness signpost translation services that are accessible to Deaf people; see www.bsltranslations.org.uk/ for more details.

The percentages of people affected by schizophrenia in the Deaf/deaf community appear to be similar to those of the general population, though it is difficult to obtain reliable data (Atkinson, 2006; Altshuler and Sarlin, 1963; Kitson and Fry, 1990; Hindley and Kitson, 2000). It is clear that many D/deaf people who are diagnosed with psychotic conditions do hear voices, though there is debate about the extent to which these are auditory.

An interesting recent development is a support group for deaf people experiencing mental health problems, set up by deaf clinical psychologist Joanna Atkinson. Atkinson (2006) found that deaf people do hear voices, but there was variation in the extent to which these could be described as audible. For example, one service user said that when he argued with a friend, he might say that his friend 'shouted' at him although auditory voices were not used.

Mood disorders

Depressive disorders

These are conditions in which low mood and self-esteem, sleep and appetite disturbances and reduced energy levels go beyond the ordinary fluctuations of mood. Sleep may be disturbed, e.g. waking early in the morning feeling worse than ever. Feelings of guilt and worthlessness can lead to despair and thoughts of self-harm and suicide. Mood levels may be different during the day (diurnal variation), e.g. feeling worse in the morning and improving during the day. If these symptoms last for more than two weeks or more, most doctors would diagnose the person as suffering from depression (Pritchard, 2006, p31). One in ten of us experience an episode of depression during our lifetime.

Mania and hypomania

These are the opposite of depression, in which elevated mood and self-esteem lead to a sense that the world is a wonderful place. If depression is the collapsing of the ego, mania is its expansion (Pritchard, 2006). Boundless energy and a speeding up of thought processes means that sleep seems unnecessary. Although energetic and good-humoured behaviour can be infectious to those around sufferers at first, grandiose behaviour such as excessive overspending and sexually disinhibited behaviour can cause difficulties in social functioning. At its most serious, psychotic symptoms such as delusions, e.g. believing that one is divine or an historical figure, may be experienced. Hypomania is a milder form of mania, which avoids the extremes of a full-blown manic episode.

Bipolar disorder (formerly known as manic-depression)

This is a disorder characterised by profound changes in mood, which may swing from periods of deep depression to periods of mania or hypomania. Some people may experience hallucinations or delusions during a manic phase. There can be long periods of stability between high or low periods.

CASE STUDY

We have already met Valerie, a 72-year-old, White British woman with a visual impairment. Her husband died six months ago and she lives alone in a rural community. When Valerie's son visited her today, she took some time to answer the door and her appearance was unkempt and tired. When her son commented that she looked tired, she said that she had difficulty getting to sleep at night and would often wake very early in the morning, feeling much worse than the night before.

When asked about what she had eaten today, Valerie said that she hadn't felt hungry. She starting crying and told him that she felt that she was a burden to him. He tried to tell her that this wasn't the case, but found it difficult to reassure her.

Comment

Valerie appears to be experiencing some of the key symptoms of depression. Her sleep patterns are disturbed, both getting to sleep at night and waking early (morning wakefulness), with her mood varying during the day (diurnal variation). Her appetite has been affected and her mood appears to be persistently low with an unrealistic sense of guilt and low self-worth. However, while the difficulties that Valerie experiences are acknowledged, again Valerie could be directed to organisations such as the Royal National Institute for Blind People (RNIB) who may be able to provide her with information and signposting for further support that she may require.

Anxiety disorders

Together with depression, anxiety disorders are the most common form of mental health problem. We all experience anxiety to some extent and it can serve a useful purpose, e.g. short-term anxiety can motivate us to prepare and perform for an exam. When levels of anxiety are considerably higher and experienced over a longer period of time, this can lead to significantly distressed and impaired functioning.

Panic attacks are intense periods of acute anxiety characterised by physical symptoms such as palpitations, rapid heart rate and nausea in which people often fear that they are having a heart attack, blacking out or going to lose control. When these are in response to specific stimuli or situations they can become phobias, e.g. agoraphobia, which is anxiety about being in situations or places where escape is difficult or embarrassing, usually alone in public places (Fortinash and Worrett, 2004).

Obsessions are persistent and intrusive thoughts or impulses that cause distress and anxiety. Compulsions are repetitive patterns of behaviour aimed at reducing anxiety. Obsessive–compulsive disorder is usually characterised by a combination of both, e.g. I may have a persistent and intrusive fear of contamination by germs and respond by washing my hands ten or twelve times in a row.

Post-traumatic stress disorder (PTSD) occurs when a traumatic event leads to intrusive and disturbing recollections of the event (flashbacks), recurrent dreams about the event and avoidance of cues that might remind the person of the event. A constant state of anxiety and sensitivity to perceived threats, e.g. jumping when a door slams, is known as hypervigilance.

Originally used to describe soldiers' experiences of combat, the term has been widened to include other traumatic events, e.g. childhood sexual abuse.

Personality disorder

Personality disorders are viewed as deeply ingrained patterns of behaviour that are maladaptive responses to situations that the person finds themselves in. There is a wide range of personality disorders with little in common. The most well-known forms are anti-social personality disorder and borderline personality disorder. Anti-social or dissocial personality disorder was previously known as psychopathy and is associated with low regard for others, irresponsible and sometimes criminal behaviour, low tolerance of frustration and a tendency to blame others. Borderline personality disorder is associated with emotional instability, intense and volatile personal relationships, poor impulse control, chronic sense of emptiness and self-destructive behaviour.

Castillo (2003) undertook a study in which user-researchers interviewed 50 people with a diagnosis of personality disorder and found a clear link between personality disorder and early trauma, with 80 per cent suffering physical, emotional and/or sexual abuse in childhood.

Personality disorder is a controversial diagnosis because of concerns that it can be used in a negative and discriminatory way to exclude people from services (Castillo, 2003). Indeed, Lewis and Appelby (1988, p44) argue that *Personality disorder appears to be an enduring pejorative term rather than a clinical diagnosis.*

This has been recognised by the Department of Health, who produced a policy document entitled *Personality disorder: No longer a diagnosis of exclusion* in 2003. This report identified the difficulties that many people with a personality diagnosis have in accessing appropriate mental health services and identifies best practice in service models and staff education and support.

Dementia

Dementia is the name of a group of diseases that cause physical changes in the brain and affect a person's intellectual functioning and memory. It is rare in people under 65, although it can affect people as young as 20. The risk increases with age, but it is not an inevitable consequence of the ageing process. Dementia affects only one in five people over 80.

The most common cause is Alzheimer's disease, which develops gradually with difficulties in short-term memory, e.g. a person not being able to remember what they were doing a few minutes ago. The second most common cause is vascular dementia, in which a series of small stokes causes damage to brain cells. Common symptoms of vascular dementia are confusion, epileptic fits and depression. While dementia may develop gradually, it can have a sudden onset often followed by a stable period. Other causes of dementia are the later stages of Parkinson's disease and Huntington's disease. There are concerns that older people experiencing depression or other conditions are being misdiagnosed with dementia (Maynard, 2003). Once again organisational support can be invaluable, with organisations such as Alzheimer Scotland providing useful advice and information for people who experience Alzheimer's as well as sensory need. For more information see www.alzscot.org/pages/info/deafness.htm.

Critique of the medical model

The medical model has received a range of criticisms. A common criticism is that it is seen as pathologising, in the sense that emotional distress is labelled as a medical problem. A related criticism is that it can be disempowering because it places service users in a passive, 'patient' role. Since it is an individualistic model, it has been seen as giving insufficient consideration to wider social factors, such as race and ethnicity, poverty and social exclusion.

Social models of mental health

The social model regards the wider influence of social forces as more important than other influences as causes or precipitants of mental health problems. Whereas other models have explanations at the level of the individual, the social model argues that symptoms should be viewed within the context of wider society and include factors such as poverty, unemployment, poor housing, discrimination and other forms of social exclusion (Tyrer and Steinberg, 1998).

It is too simplistic to talk of a single 'social model', because there is a range of different social models of mental health. However, they are all based on the premise that social influences are vital for understanding mental health and illness.

Labelling theory

Labelling theory challenges the medical model by arguing that the concept of mental illness is socially constructed as a means of categorising and controlling behaviour that we are not able to understand and which does not correspond with another category of deviant behaviour, e.g. crime. Just as people with mental health can be labelled, so can people with sensory need, thus again highlighting the complexities of the combination of mental health and sensory need. Labelling theory argues that, once someone has been labelled as 'mentally ill', this can be self-reinforcing, e.g. there is a tendency for previous and future behaviour to be interpreted in the light of the psychiatric diagnosis. It was first developed as a general theory of deviant behaviour by the sociologist Howard Becker, who argued that society labels people in a way that defines them as a particular kind of individual. It is not a neutral label, but involves judgements about the person in which he or she is assumed to have all of the supposed negative qualities of a wider group, e.g. 'criminal', 'mad person'. The person then is responded to by others relating to the label rather than their individual characteristics.

The theory was applied to the mental health field by Thomas Scheff in his classic text, *Being mentally ill* (1966). Scheff (1996) suggests there are two reactions to deviant behaviour: denial or labelling. Denial 'normalises' the rule-breaking by ignoring or rationalising it. When this happens the deviant behaviour is likely to end or be channelled into a socially acceptable form. However, when someone is labelled, the deviance is confirmed and the rule-breaking behaviour continues as the person conforms to the label. For example, a service user developed acute symptoms of schizophrenia every time he had money worries, rather than asking for help or recognising his own ability to solve his own problems. So the labelling as 'schizophrenic' and the treatment which followed from it could be seen as a self-fulfilling prophecy. More recently, Scheff (1999) has argued that he presented a sociological account of mental illness that was an effective critique of psychiatry, but this is only a partial account that requires integration with more mainstream perspectives. As a critique of psychiatry, the consequences of being labelled as 'mentally ill' were most clearly demonstrated in a classic study by David Rosenhan (1973).

On being sane in insane places

Rosenhan (1973) completed a classic study into the impact of labelling in mental health services. In the study, eight people who had no psychiatric history presented at psychiatric hospitals in various locations in the United States and claimed that they were hearing voices which said 'empty', 'hollow' and 'thud'. The group of 'pseudo-patients' consisted of three psychologists, a psychiatrist, a paediatrician, a painter, a housewife and a graduate psychology student. No other symptoms were reported and participants otherwise described their own history and circumstances. All of the participants were admitted into hospital, seven with a diagnosis of schizophrenia and one with a diagnosis of manic depression.

As soon as they were admitted to hospital, participants stopped showing any psychiatric symptoms, said that they no longer heard voices and behaved as they would normally. Initially, participants wrote their research notes in their rooms, but soon realised that they could write these on the ward. One participant later requested their nursing notes, which stated, 'Patient engaging in writing behaviour', which was seen as being linked to their illness. At no point were the pseudo-patients detected by staff, but many were suspected by other patients. Their average stay in hospital was 19 days, but this ranged from 7 to 52 days. All were discharged with the diagnosis of 'schizophrenia in remission'.

Rosenhan (1973) argued that psychiatry could not tell the difference between 'sane' and 'insane' behaviour and concluded that once someone has received a psychiatric label, all of their behaviour is then interpreted in terms of the diagnosis. Obviously, the study raised a number of ethical issues about how research should be conducted but it provided a thought-provoking critique of psychiatry.

Stigma, discrimination and anti-discriminatory practice

As already highlighted in Chapter 3, stigma and discriminatory attitudes towards people with sensory needs have a long history. The example was highlighted that under ancient Roman law, deaf people were classified as *mentecatti furiosi* (literally, 'raving maniacs') and were claimed to be 'uneducable' (Gracer, 2003). When taking into account the level of stigma and discrimination a person with sensory needs may already experience, it is all the more important for you to appreciate issues experienced by people who have both sensory and mental health needs. It is also important to note that stigma and discrimination can be intensified further if a person additionally experiences prejudice in relation to a range of factors, such as race, age, culture, sexual orientation and gender.

There is evidence that people with mental health problems face significant levels of stigma and discrimination (Green et al., 2003). This discrimination can lead to people with mental health problems internalising negative beliefs, which can lead to low self-esteem and social consequences such as difficulties in employment and relationships. The labelling process described above can mean that when, for example, someone feels justifiably angry, this may be interpreted by others as a 'symptom' of their illness.

When people are already part of a group who experience discrimination, the effects can be multiplied. This has been most clearly documented in relation to race, gender and sexual orientation.

'Race' and mental health

There is significant evidence that people from black and minority ethnic (BME) communities face discrimination in mental health services. For example, while the total BME population in the UK is 8 per cent, more than 40 per cent of people detained on a compulsory basis were recorded as 'mixed', 'black' or 'black British' (Health and Social Care Information Centre, 2008). Patients from BME communities are more likely to be treated in hospital rather than in the community, to receive restrictive measures such as seclusion in hospital and to come into contact with services through the criminal justice system (Department of Health, 2005).

A number of explanations have been identified for these inequalities. Firstly, one explanation is that psychiatry itself is Eurocentric in the sense that it is based upon a Western conception of what is 'normal', which is influenced by imperialist assumptions about the biological, moral and intellectual inferiority of non-Western cultures (Fernando, 2001). Indeed, Fernando (1988) has argued that psychiatry grew as a discipline when colonisation and slavery were at their height and contains implicit notions that white people, behaviour and social norms are superior. A second explanation draws upon a growing body of literature which suggests that poverty, racism, social exclusion, poor education and unemployment create an increased risk of developing mental health problems and that this is especially so in ethnic minority communities. A third explanation is that institutional racism is endemic in mental health services themselves, e.g. a 'culture-blind' approach that purports to treat everybody the same but actually is orientated towards meeting the needs of white European service users. Another variation is where there is ethnic stereotyping, e.g. 'Asian families look after their own family members' as an explanation for low uptake of services, rather than considering whether certain communities are excluded from services.

Gender and mental health

Women are approximately twice as likely to experience anxiety and depression and two to three times as likely to self-harm, e.g. cutting, burning and overdose (Department of Health, 2002). Some mental health conditions are specific to women, e.g. postnatal depression, which affects at least one new mother in ten (Mind, 2006).

As in the relationship between mental health, race and culture, similar processes appear to underpin the relationship between gender and mental health. For example, behaviour defined as 'male' is seen by psychiatrists to be congruent with healthy behaviour, while behaviour defined as 'female' is not (Broverman et al., 1970). This might mean a small amount of aggression may be tolerated from men, but women are more likely to find that showing aggression will be regarded as pathological.

The impact of life events

One model that provides a bridge between medical and social models of mental health is the life events model. This model believes that people are particularly vulnerable during key events or transitions in their lives. It is widely accepted within psychiatry but also gives considerable weight to social rather than biological factors. We shall focus on the experience of bereavement as an example of how life events can affect our mental health.

Loss and bereavement

Issues of loss and bereavement are central to understanding the impact of life events on mental health. In Chapter 4, loss and bereavement were explored in relation to sensory need. In this section, we shall look at two models that you were introduced to in Chapter 4, a classic model and a more recent model to demonstrate our growing understanding of this field, but we shall apply it mainly to the field of mental health.

The first model that we shall look at is from the work of Kübler-Ross (1970), who conducted a well-known observational study of people who had received a terminal diagnosis. Although originally intended as a study on the process of dying, it has also become known as a model for understanding grief (Currer, 2007). Five stages of grief were identified.

- *Denial* A common reaction to bad news is disbelief, a sense that it cannot be true.

- *Anger* Feelings of anger can be linked to a sense of 'How can this happen?' People may feel that someone must be blamed.

- *Bargaining* Characterised by a sense of wanting to negotiate with fate for some control, e.g. living until a specific event, such as a wedding or birth.

- *Depression* Once the future has begun to be accepted, this can lead to sadness and possibly guilt and unworthiness.

- *Acceptance* Although happiness and contentment may not be experienced, a sense of resolution marks the end of active struggle (Currer, 2007).

This model has undergone considerable development from the original model but has remained influential in understanding bereavement. One of the main criticisms it has attracted is that it implies that everyone should pass through all of the phases in a particular order. This does not reflect the complex experiences of bereaved people and can be rather rigid and prescriptive (Walsh, 2007).

More recent models of loss and bereavement have been influenced by developments in sociological theories which focus on our sense of identity and how it is constructed. They argue that our sense of self is created through social interaction with others, in which the response that we receive from others helps build our sense of who we are and influences how we behave. These approaches are called narrative approaches because our lives are viewed as having 'storylines'. When these storylines are disturbed by the experience of loss, we have to reauthor our lives in line with the new reality (Currer, 2007).

The second model we shall discuss derives from this tradition. Walter (1996) presents his 'new model of grief', which addresses criticisms of earlier theories and argues that the purpose of grief is to sustain the link with the lost person rather than to 'move on' (Currer, 2007, p68). He highlights the views of many bereaved people that they do not want to move on from their loved one. The experience of loss means that the nature of the bond has to change but it is a matter of relocating the loved one rather than leaving them behind.

CASE STUDY

In one of our case studies, we met Valerie, a 72-year-old white British woman whose husband died six months ago after an extended illness, and who lives alone in a rural community. Her eyesight has been deteriorating for some time and she no longer feels safe to drive, which severely restricts her ability to get out. Her son lives nearby and tries to visit as often as he can but he has his own family. He has noticed that his mother seems low in mood and she and her home look increasingly unkempt. She does not show her usual pleasure in cooking, saying that 'she can't be bothered'.

Although her husband had suffered an extended illness, his death came as a significant shock to Valerie. Once she had got over the initial shock and disbelief, she found that she felt anger towards her husband's GP because she felt that he 'had not done enough' for her husband. All the family had been very supportive at the funeral and for a while afterwards. However, that was six months ago and she felt that everything had returned to normal for everyone but herself. Her son came round when he could, but she felt very guilty when he visited because 'he has a family of his own' so she found difficulty in enjoying his visits.

ACTIVITY 6.2

How might the theories we have looked at help us to understand Valerie's experiences?

Comment

Valerie has experienced a number of losses. Firstly, she has been recently widowed. This can have a devastating impact for many people with significant psychological and social consequences. Secondly, her eyesight is deteriorating, resulting in her not feeling safe to drive. In a geographically isolated, rural community this could lead to significant difficulties in her everyday life and potentially lead to social isolation. In Chapter 4, we discussed two types of loss: that of finite loss, which is the type of loss used to describe death, as in the case of Valerie losing her husband in death; and non-finite loss, that of Valerie losing her eyesight (Bruce and Shultz, 2001; Currer, 2007). The case study of Valerie highlights the impact loss and bereavement can have on a person's life and again highlights the need for individualised practice.

We can see some aspects of the different stages suggested by Kübler-Ross's model. Yet it is important that we do not apply theoretical models in a rigid and deterministic way. The model was developed to describe common patterns in the ways that people deal with loss, not as a prescriptive model of how people 'should' grieve. In your practice, you need to recognise and value uniqueness of individual experiences, rather than expecting that people experiencing loss will express their grief in predetermined ways.

Legislation, policy and services

Most people with mental health problems receive services through primary care, e.g. GP surgeries. A minority of people with more complex needs are referred by their GP on to specialist services, which can range from a Community Mental Health Team to a hospital in-patient unit.

Community Mental Health Teams (CMHTs) are multi-disciplinary teams comprising professionals from a range of backgrounds, usually social work, nursing, psychiatry, psychology and occupational therapy. People experiencing a severe and enduring mental illness would normally be allocated a CMHT team member who acts as a central point for co-ordinating any services that the person receives under the Care Programme Approach (CPA). CPA is a national framework for ensuring that the services received by each service user are co-ordinated effectively. Another key milestone in service development was the National Service Framework (NSF) for Mental Health, which was published in 1999. This set national standards and introduced national targets for health promotion and addressing discrimination for the first time as part of a wider commitment to tackling social exclusion.

When people are experiencing an acute crisis, it can be appropriate for them to be admitted into hospital. Of those people admitted into hospital, 80 per cent receive treatment on a voluntary basis. The remaining 20 per cent are compulsory or formal patients under the Mental Health Act 1983, which has been amended by the Mental Health Act 2007. These acts provide a legislative framework for the compulsory detention of people suffering from a mental disorder that warrants detention in the interests of their own health or safety, or with a view to protecting others. An essential aspect to consider when working with a person who has mental health needs is that of communication, as highlighted in Chapter 2. Admission into hospital, whether it is voluntary or compulsory, can be a frightening experience. Consequently, it is essential that a person with sensory needs receives access to appropriate communication. For example, the person may need a lipspeaker, a sign language interpreter or a deafblind manual communicator. If an appropriate communication method is not provided, the mental health assessment may be inaccurate as the necessary information may be inaccurately conveyed or received.

CASE STUDY

Several days ago, Ronnie was detained under the Mental Health Act 1983. He was observed taking his clothes off in a supermarket late one evening and the police were called. He was very excited and disinhibited, signing that he felt 'at one with nature' and that clothes felt very restrictive.

Section 136 of the Mental Health Act 1983 gives a police officer the power to take to a place of safety any person who is in a public place who appears to be 'suffering from mental disorder' and is 'in immediate need of care or control'. This power lasts up to 72 hours and enables the person to be assessed under the Act. Under this section, Ronnie was taken to the place of safety suite at the local mental health unit, which was part of the general hospital.

continued

Given that Ronnie has a sensory need it was felt that the arrangements for him being assessed under the Mental Health Act were particularly important so he was provided with access to a sign language interpreter so his wishes and feelings were made known and he was kept overnight. Next day, his GP and social worker from the sensory team were contacted to be part of the assessment. It was established that British Sign Language was Ronnie's preferred means of communicating so a BSL interpreter was arranged.

The assessment was co-ordinated by a sensory social worker who had completed additional training to become an Approved Mental Health Professional (AMHP). She assessed Ronnie as did a psychiatrist who had completed specialist training, and Ronnie's GP. Both doctors recommended that it was appropriate for Ronnie to be detained in hospital but it is the Approved Mental Health Professional who makes the decision whether or not he should be detained. Since Ronnie was not previously known to mental health services, he was detained under section 2 of the Mental Health Act 1983, which means he can be detained for up to 28 days for assessment. For further information on mental health legislation and policy, please see Johns (2009) and Barber et al. (2008). Throughout the process Ronnie had access to a British Sign Language interpreter.

Mental health and deafness

There is an established link between deafness and mental health problems. For example, 25 per cent of children are likely to experience mental health problems but this rises to 40 per cent for deaf children. There are a number of studies from different countries that suggest that it is similar for adults (DoH, 2005).

The difficulties that deaf people with mental health problems experience in accessing services have been longstanding, but were highlighted in 2000 with the independent inquiry report into the care of Daniel Joseph, an 18-year-old, deaf man with mental health problems. Daniel had been charged with manslaughter on the grounds of diminished responsibility after attacking two women, one of whom later died from her injuries. The inquiry concluded that mental health services for deaf people do not receive the priority that they warrant. Specific recommendations were that mental health assessments of deaf people should normally involve a sign language interpreter and mental health professionals should receive training in working with deaf people and interpreters as part of their basic training.

Concerns over the care received by Daniel Joseph led to a government review of mental health services for deaf people, published by the Department of Health as a consultation paper, *A sign of the times: Modernising mental health services for people who are deaf*, in 2002. This consultation document led to best practice guidance, entitled *Mental health and deafness: Towards equity and access* (DoH, 2005). The guidance made a number of key recommendations.

- Consideration should be given to conducting local needs assessments of the mental health of deaf people.

- Primary care and hospital trusts to include deaf awareness training for all front-line staff.

115

- Every primary care facility should have a minicom and a service agreement with a translation service which includes BSL.

- Staff working in mental health settings should be encouraged to learn BSL and consideration should be given to the recruitment of specialist Community Psychiatric Nurses (CPNs).

- Mental health trusts involved in providing services in prisons should identify deaf prisoners with mental health problems.

- The number of Deaf people employed in mental health services at all levels should be increased (DoH, 2005).

There have also been significant developments in the voluntary sector. Specific organisations and services for people with sensory needs who experience mental health problems are relatively new. For example, the British Society for Mental Health and Deafness was formed in 1994 to campaign to increase sensory awareness and improve services to deaf people with mental health problems, e.g. working to develop British Sign Language versions of standardised mental health assessment tools such as the Beck Depression Inventory.

C H A P T E R   S U M M A R Y

In this chapter, we have considered how mental health problems have been understood and we have identified a range of controversies in the mental health field which have centred on the distinction between medical and social models. You have been introduced to the main forms of mental health problems, as defined with a medical model. We have explored a number of social models, which argue that social factors have a strong influence on how mental health problems are identified and responded to. Finally, we have discussed how people with sensory needs may experience additional barriers to accessing appropriate services; the importance of appropriate communicative provision; and identified key measures that can be helpful.

FURTHER READING

Currer, C (2007) *Loss and social work.* Exeter: Learning Matters.

An excellent account of theoretical development around loss, change and grieving. A highly relevant book for a wide range of social work settings as social work interventions are often used to support service users struggling with issues of loss.

Golightley, M (2008) *Social work and mental health.* Third edition. Exeter: Learning Matters.

The third edition of this popular textbook, updated to include the Mental Health Act 2007 and the Mental Capacity Act 2005. Comes from a clear social work perspective and addresses values and ethical issues as well as legislative and policy contexts.

Mind (National Association for Mental Health) www.mind.org.uk

Influential national organisation, which campaigns and provides services to promote a better life for people experiencing mental health problems. Set up in 1948, its campaigns led to the Mental Health Act 1983 and its national network of services provided a major impetus for service user involvement in the UK.

British Society for Mental Health and Deafness (BSMHD) www.bsmhd.org.uk

A voluntary organisation formed in 1994 to campaign to increase sensory awareness and improve services to deaf people with mental health problems. Includes professionals and organisations whose work impacts on deaf people experiencing mental health problems. Aims to promote good practice and service innovation, e.g. currently working to develop British Sign Language versions of standardised mental health assessment tools such as the Beck Depression Inventory.

Glickman, NS and Sanjay G (eds) (2003) *Mental health care of deaf people: A culturally affirmative approach*. Philadelphia, PA: Lawrence Erlbaum Associates.

An interesting and useful edited collection that covers deaf children as well as adults. Includes discussion of communication strategies and the importance of culturally affirmative practice.

Conclusion

The aim of this book is to raise awareness in all aspects of sensory need in relation to social work practice. Social work is a complex role by the very nature of the fact that we work with humans who are often unpredictable and, when additional needs arise, so does potential for further complexities. While a range of sensory needs has been covered, including Deafness/deafness, visual impairment and deafblindness, the intention has been to highlight that fundamental principles remain the same when working with an adult or a child with any sensory need.

This book has emphasised that various factors are essential to ensure good practice. These include:

- considering individuality and development of your own practice;
- considering the individuality of the service user, parent or carer themselves;
- considering the importance of appropriate service user involvement.

The book has also highlighted that while these complexities can occur, it is possible with simple practical techniques, patience and creativity to redress the balance.

Chapter 1 began with an overview of key definitions clarifying what is meant by sensory need. Clear comprehension of this is essential in order to begin working with someone with a sensory need. This will enable you as a worker to have insight into sensory needs of the people you work with.

As was highlighted, while some people will regard sensory need as a disability, this will not be the case with all people. However, although it is important to respect the wishes of people who do not want their sensory difference seen as a disability, it is equally important to respect the views of a person if they do perceive themselves as having a disability.

We have continually highlighted throughout this book the need to recognise and respect cultural diversity and difference; anti-discriminatory practice; recognition of risk and taking appropriate action; using theories, models and legislation to underpin practice; use of critical and analytical reflection and thinking; using appropriate communication methods; use of technology and the essentiality of being creative.

There is continual emphasis from the General Social Care Council, Children's Workforce Development Council and other key organisations on continuous professional development. As was highlighted in Chapters 4 and 5, this is especially important when working with vulnerable groups such as children and vulnerable adults. There is a need to learn from insight, for example analysing and critically thinking on serious case reviews and reflecting on associated literature and research.

The final chapter was dedicated to sensory awareness and mental health and looked at issues faced by people with mental health issues in relation to sensory need. Understanding and empathic practice is essential when a person has a range of complex needs in addition to their sensory need. However, once again this requires understanding and sensitivity, taking into account service user wishes and balancing these with risk (GSCC, 2001).

As students and practitioners we will never understand everything associated with sensory need. We will find that as 'students of life' we will be constantly learning new things. As authors we want this book to raise sensory awareness not only within the field of social work but within all professional roles. We hope this book has been a starting point for those of you who are new to the social care field or a useful resource for those of you who are more experienced.

Throughout this book we have referred to other titles in the Learning Matters Transforming Social Work Practice series. We hope this book and the other titles will be a useful resource not only now but as you continue to develop professionally as a practitioner.

Resources and organisations

Blind/Partially sighted

American Blind Athletic Organization [online] Available at: www.usaba.org/

Audio Description [online] Available at: www.audiodescription.com

Equipment and other support to enable blind or visually impaired people to live independently at home. [online] Available at: www.direct.gov.uk/en/DisabledPeople/

Guide Dogs *for Blind/Partially Sighted People* [online] Available at: www.guidedogs.org.uk/

Metropolitan Society for the Blind [online] Available at: www.glfb.org.uk/main/metropolitan.html

National Blind Children Society [online] Available at: www.nbcs.org.uk

RNIB Braille [online] Available at: www.rnib.org.uk/xpedio/groups/public/documents/publicwebsite/public_louisbraille.hcsp

Royal National Institute for the Blind RNIB [online] Available at: www.rnib.org.uk. 105 Judd Street, London, WC1H 9NE. Tel: 020 7388 1266 / 0303 123 9999 or Fax: 020 7388 2034.

Sighted Guide Techniques. For information [online] Available at: www.brailleinstitute. org/docs/SightedGuideTechniques – *For further information in your local area contact local authority or RNIB [online} Available at:* www.rnib.org.uk

The Organisation of blind Africans & Caribbean's OBAC [online] Available at: www.obac. org.uk/ 'OBAC exists to ensure blind and partially sighted Africans and Caribbean people access relevant services, influence decision and policy makers, to enable them to overcome barriers that prevent them become active members of the community' (OBAC 2009).

Deaf/deaf/deafened and hard of hearing

BDA – British Deaf Association [online] Available at: bda.org.uk/British_Deaf_Association-i-34.html

Connevans – Equipment for deaf and hearing impaired people in education, employment, the home and leisure [online] Available at: www.connevans.com or sales@connevans.com

Cued Articulation [online] Available at: www.cuedarticulationtraining.com

Cued Speech [online] Available at: www.cuedspeech.co.uk/
Hearing Concern LINK provide support to people with a hearing loss and their families. [online] Available at: www.hearingconcernlink.org/ 356 Holloway Road, London, N7 6PA Tel: 020 7700 8177. Text: 020 7700 8177. Fax: 020 7700 8211.

Hearing Dogs for Deaf People [online] Available at: www.hearingdogs.org.uk

Interpreter's for People who are Deaf/deaf Deaf people have the right to have a qualified interpreter for medical appointments etc. [online] Available at: www.direct.gov.uk/en/DisabledPeople

Makaton [online] Available at: www.makaton.org

National Deaf Children Society (NDCS) 15 Dufferin Street, London EC1Y 8UR. Tel: 0808 800 8880 (voice or text). E-mail: helpline@ndcs.org.uk. Tel: 0808 800 8880 – The NDCS provide an equipment loan service. 'The Blue Peter Loan Service was set up in 1985 following a successful television appeal by the popular children's programme. The service offers deaf children and their families throughout the UK the opportunity to borrow radio aids and other equipment to try in the comfort of their own homes or at school. If a child has borrowed the equipment and gets benefit from it, they may be able to obtain the equipment from their local education authority or social services. The NDCS may be able to help the family with this' (NDCS 2009). For details of NDCS equipment loan service contact helpline.

Paget Gorman sign system [online] Available at: www.pgss.org/

Pictorial Exchange Communication System (PECS) [online] Available at: www.pecs.org.uk/general/what.htm

RNID [online] Available at: www.rnid.org.uk/ 19–23 Featherstone Street, London EC1Y 8SL. Tel: 020 7296 8000. Text: 020 7296 8001. Fax: 020 7296 8199.

RNID [online] Available at: www.informationline@rnid.org.uk

Research on the Violation of Human Rights of Deaf People in Mozambique By Francisco Manuel Tembe (famod@kepa.co.mz) [online] Available at: www.disabilityworld.org/11-12_01/il/mozambique.shtml

Sarabec – Equipment provision [online] Available at: www.sarabec.com

Signalong [online] Available at : www.signalong.org.uk

Deafblind

Communicator Guide Provision – Advice and information from SENSE [online] Available at: www.sense.org.uk or Deafblind UK[online] Available at: www.deafblind.org.uk

Deafblind UK 2008 [online] Available at: www.deafblind.org.uk Supports children and adults who are deafblind. Tel: 0800 132 320.

Deafblind UK Equipment Provision and Advice [online] Available at: www.deafblind.co.uk/equipment.html

Intervenor Provision – Advice and information from SENSE [online] Available at: www.sense.org.uk

SENSE [online] Available at: www.sense.org.uk Supports children and adults who are deafblind. 101 Pentonville Road, London N1 9LG. Tel: 0845 127 0060. Text: 0845 127 0062. Fax : 0845 127 0061. E mail: info@sense.org.uk

SENSE (2007) *Seeing me. Fill in the gaps*, June, pp1–25.

Usher Information – www.nidcd.nih.gov/health/hearing/usher.asp

General sensory resources

Aspergers Support – The National Autistic Society [online] Available at: www.nas.org.uk/ asperger

Autism – The National Autistic Society [online] Available at: www.nas.org.uk/autism

CACDP is an online directory containing details of Language Service Professionals (LSP) who have met the national standards for their profession. These include BSL/English interpreters, Lipspeakers, Speech to Text Reporters, LSPs – Deafblind Manual and Electronic or Manual Notetakers. [online] Available at: www.cacdp.org.uk/interpreters/online.../online-directory.html

Disability Discrimination Act 1995/2005 is legislation which promotes civil rights for disabled people and protects disabled people from discrimination [online] Available at: www.direct.gov.uk/en/DisabledPeople.

Legislation

Great Britain. Local Authority Social Services Act 1970. London: HMSO

Great Britain. Children Act 1989/04. London: HMSO

Great Britain. National Health Service and Community Care Act 1990. London: HMSO

Great Britain. Disability Discrimination Act 1995/2005. London: HMSO

Great Britain. The Community Care (Direct Payments) Act 1996. London: HMSO

Great Britain. Education Act 1996. London: HMSO

Great Britain. Care Standards Act 2000. London: HMSO

Great Britain. Special Educational Needs and Disability Act 2001. London: HMSO

Great Britain. Education Act 2002. London: HMSO.

Glossary

Acquired sensory loss the development of sensory loss, after previously having the sense.

Anosmia the lack of the ability or the inability to smell.

Audiologist a person who will test hearing and advise on best course of action for hearing loss.

Audiology the study of hearing, balance, and related hearing disorders.

Blind/severely sight impaired inability to see due to psychological, physical or neurological factors.

Block communication is conveyed by drawing capital letters onto the palm of the visually impaired/deafblind person. As with deafblind manual there is a pause in between words.

Bold print format bold outline and or large font size. This is personalised to each individual.

Braille a tactile system of writing in which patterns of raised dots represent letters and numerals.

British Sign Language (BSL) a visual means of communication using signs. It has its own grammatical structure and syntax and is recognised as an official language in its own right. Contrary to belief, BSL is regional and sign language varies.

Capital 'D' Deaf person a person who considers themselves to be Deaf would most likely be a profoundly deaf person who would not consider themselves to be disabled, but rather part of a minority group with their own culture, history and linguistics (British Deaf Association, 2007). This was highlighted by the BDA when British Sign Language (BSL) attained official language status on 18 March 2003. Deaf people consider being Deaf as part of their heritage and most likely consider themselves proud to be Deaf.

CHARGE syndrome a genetic disorder. CHARGE was the acronym used to describe the associated features of the syndrome, which were:

- C – coloboma (congenital anomaly in which some of the structure of the eye is absent) of the eye.
- H – heart defect.
- A – atresia (a condition in which an opening or tube in the body is closed or absent) of the choanae (posterior nasal aperture).
- R – retardation of development/growth.
- G – genital/urinary anomalies.
- E – ear anomalies/deafness.

While these features no longer appear to be directly used in sole diagnosis, the acronym remains the same.

Clear speech use of clear speech, light and environment to enhance the sound quality of the speech.

Communication passports outline personalised communication used by each individual child/adult. Examples of people who may use a communication passport are a person who has a learning need or one who has a sensory need such as deafblindness.

Congenital existing from birth.

Cued articulation used in education, this is a set of hand cues for teaching the individual sounds in a word. It is not sign language, however: each hand movement represents one sound and the cue gives clues as to how and where the sound is produced.

Cued speech uses eight hand-shapes in four different positions near the mouth to clarify the lip patterns of normal speech.

Deafened to become deaf or hard of hearing due to exposure to loud noise. This can be permanent or temporary.

Deafblind combined visual and hearing difficulties. Most people have some useful hearing and/or sight. Some individuals may experience profound sight and hearing loss. As with the word 'Deaf', it can be capitalised to indicate there is a culture.

Deafblind manual alphabet the alphabet is similar to that of BSL but is communicated directly onto the hand of the visually impaired/deafblind person. Each letter is placed over the top of the last. There is a pause in between words to indicate that a new word has started.

Dysgeusia the distortion or decrease of the sense of taste.

Glaucoma an eye condition involving a group of diseases of the optic nerve.

Hands-on signing a communication method based upon British Sign Language enabling the person to feel the signs. With this system, the deafblind person follows the signs by placing his hands over those of the signer and feeling the signs produced.

Hard of hearing a person who cannot hear sounds to their maximum potential. A person can be born hard of hearing or acquire it as they become more advanced in years.

Lipreader/lipreading a person who uses a lipspeaker as an interpreter and reads the lips of the lipspeaker to acquire the information conveyed.

Lipspeaking a lipspeaker is a hearing person who makes sure they are clearly visible to the lipreader and silently and accurately repeats the spoken message.

Loop the loop system is a device which enables people with a hearing loss to obtain maximum involvement in communication in the environment in which the loop is fitted. The loop has a microphone, an amplifier and loop wire which is installed around the area in which the person sits. The receiver would usually be the person's hearing aid. The hearing aid would be set to the 'T' position, or cinema position as children tend to call it.

Makaton a simplified form of sign language using simple hand signs. Often used with people who have a learning disability. Makaton uses symbols to support the written word.

Meningococcal infection a germ. While infection with the meningococcus is uncommon, it is very serious. It can cause meningitis and/or septicaemia.

Moon a code of raised shapes which enables people who are visually impaired/deafblind to read by touch.

Oralism oralists educate d/Deaf students using spoken language consisting of lipreading, speech, the process of watching mouth movements, and mastering breathing techniques.

Paget Gorman a grammatical sign system which reflects normal patterns of English.

Partially sighted/sight impaired a person whose vision limits visual capability.

PECS Pictorial Exchange Communication System.

Residual sensory loss – remaining and useful.

Retinitis pigmentosa (RP) genetic eye condition, which may incorporate night blindness and tunnel vision.

Signalong a sign supporting system based on British Sign Language. It is being used increasingly to support individuals with communication difficulties as part of a total communication approach.

Signed Supported English (SSE) a visual means of communication using signs in English word structure.

Small 'd' deaf person a deaf person is likely to have been a previously hearing person or one who was born deaf, growing up in a hearing family with oral communication being the primary means of communication. A person who has previously experienced the ability to hear music, voices and birds singing and then becomes profoundly deaf, for example as a result of meningococcal infection, can experience this as a quite traumatic loss and be more likely to label themselves with a disability.

Tadoma a method of communication primarily used by people who are deafblind. The deafblind person places their thumb on the speaker's lips and their fingers along the speaker's jaw line. The middle three fingers often fall along the speaker's cheeks with the little finger picking up the vibrations of the speaker's throat.

Usher syndrome a rare inherited disorder that is a leading cause of deafblindness. Usher syndrome is primarily characterised by deafness due to an impaired ability of the auditory nerves to transmit sensory input to the brain (sensorineural hearing loss) accompanied by retinitis pigmentosa, a degeneration of the retinal cells that can cause progressive loss of central and peripheral vision.

References

Adams, R, Dominelli, L and Payne, M (2002) *Social work themes, issues and critical debates*. Second edition. Basingstoke: Palgrave.

Ainsworth, MDS (1973) The development of infant-mother attachment. In Caldwell, BM and Ricciuti, HN (eds) *Review of child development research*, Vol. 3. Chicago, IL: University of Chicago Press.

Ainsworth, MD, Blehar, M, Alters, E and Wall, S (1978) *Patterns of attachment: A psychological study of the strange situation*. Hillsdale, NJ: Lawrence Erlbaum Associates.

Alderson, P (2001) Prenatal screening, ethics and Down's syndrome: A literature review. *Nursing Ethics*, 8 (4), 360–71.

Altshuler, K and Sarlin, M (1963) Deafness and schizophrenia: A family study. In Rainer, J, Altshuler, M, Kallmann, F and Deming E (eds) *Family and mental health problems in a deaf population*. New York: Columbia University Press, pp204–13.

American Psychiatric Association (2000) *Diagnostic and statistical manual of mental disorders*, Version IV. Washington, DC: American Psychiatric Association.

Anderson, P (2001) Pre-natal screening, ethics and Down syndrome. *Nursing Ethics*, 8(4), 360–74.

Association of Directors of Adult Social Services (2009) *Putting people first; Measuring progress* [online] Available at: **www.adass.org.uk**

Atkinson, J (2006) The perceptual characteristics of voice-hallucinations in deaf people: Insights into the nature of subvocal thought and sensory feedback loops. *Schizophrenia Bulletin*, 32 (4), 701–8.

Banks, S (2006) *Ethics and values in social work*. Third edition. Basingstoke: Palgrave Macmillan.

Barber, P, Brown, R and Martin, D (2008) *Mental health law in England and Wales.* Exeter: Learning Matters.

Barker, RL (2003) *The social work dictionary*. Fifth edition. Washington DC: NASW Press.

Bateman, N (2000) *Advocacy skills for health and social care professionals*. London: Jessica Kingsley.

Bernard, C (1999) Child sexual abuse and the black disabled child. *Disability and Society*, 14 (3), 325–39.

Bernstein, CM (2007) Introduction to dual sensory loss issue. *Trends in Amplification*, 11 (4), 217–18.

Best, H (1943) *Deafness and the deaf in the United States*. New York: Macmillan.

Bourdieu, P (1991) *Language and symbolic power*. Cambridge: Polity Press.

Bower, M (ed) (2005) *Psychoanalytic theory for social work practice: Thinking under fire*. Abingdon: Routledge.

Bowlby, J (1988) *A secure base: clinical application of attachment theory*. London: Routledge.

Bowlby, J (1973) *Attachment and loss: Vol. 2 Separation, anxiety and anger.* New York: Basic Books.

Bowlby, J (1969) *Attachment and loss: Vol. 1 Attachment*. New York: Basic Books.

Brabyn, JA, Schneck, ME, Haegerstrom-Portnoy, G, and Lott, LA (2007) Dual sensory loss: overview of problems, visual assessment and rehabilitation. *Trends of Amplification*, 11 (4), 219–26.

Brayne, H and Carr, H (2005) *Law for social workers*. Ninth edition. Oxford: Oxford University Press.

British Council of Disabled People (BCODP) **www.bcodp.org.uk**

British Deaf Association www.bda.org.uk

Bronfenbrenner, U (1979) Contexts of child rearing: problems and prospects. *American Psychologist*, 34, 844–50.

Bronfenbrenner, U (1979) *The ecology of human development*. Cambridge, MA: Harvard University Press.

Broverman, IK, Broverman, DM, Clarkson, FE, Rosenkrantz, PS and Vogel, SR (1970) Sex-role stereotypes and clinical judgments of mental health. *Journal of Consulting and Clinical Psychology*, 34(1): 1–7.

Brown, K and Rutter, L (2006) *Critical thinking for social work.* Exeter: Learning Matters.

Bruce, EJ and Schultz, CL (2001) *Non-finite loss and grief*. London: Jessica Kingsley.

Cabinet Office (2005) The Prime Minister's Strategy Unit report – Improving the life chances of disabled people: Strategy Unit [online] Available at: **www.cabinetoffice.gov.uk**

Campbell, J and Oliver, M (2006) *Disability politics.* Abingdon: Routledge.

Carey, M (2003) Anatomy of a care manager. *Work, Employment and Society,* 17,121–8.

Castillo, H (2003) *Personality disorder: Temperament or trauma?* London: Jessica Kingsley.

Children's Workforce Development Council (CWDC) (2005) Available online at: **www.cwdcouncil.org.uk**

Chou, K-L and Chi, I (2004) The combined effect of vision and hearing impairment on depression in elderly Chinese. *International Journal of Geriatric Psychiatry*: 19 (9), 825–32.

Collins, C (2008) That's not my child anymore! Parental grief after acquired brain injury ABIO: Incidence, nature and longevity. *British Journal of Social Work,* 38(8),1499–517.

Community Care (Article) (2005) [online] Available at: **www.communitycare.co.uk/**

Community Care Statistics referrals, assessments and packages of care for adults, England: National Report and CSSR tabled. NHS The information Centre for Health and Social Care (2004/2005 /2006) [online] Available at: **www.ic.nhs.uk/statistics-and-data-collections/**.

Congress, EP (2004) Cultural and ethical issues in working with culturally diverse patients and their families: The use of the culturagram to promote cultural competent practice in health care settings. *Social Work in Health Care*, 39(3–4), 249–62.

Cooley, CH (1902) Human nature and the social order. New York: Scribner. In Thompson, N (2003) *Communication and language. A handbook of theory and practice*. Basingstoke: Palgrave Macmillan.

Crawford, K and Walker, J (2007) *Social work and human development*. Second edition. Exeter: Learning Matters.

Crawford, K and Walker, J (2004) *Social work and human development*. Exeter: Learning Matters.

Cree, EV and Macaulay, C (2000) *Transfer of learning in professional vocational education*. London: Routledge.

Cross, M (1998) *Proud child, safer child: A handbook for parents and carers of disabled children*. London: Women's Press.

Currer, C (2007) *Loss and social work*. Exeter: Learning Matters.

Dawson, C (2000) *Independent successes: Implementing direct payments*. York: Joseph Rowntree Foundation.

D'Ardenne, P and Mahtani, A (1999) *Transcultural counselling in action*. Second edition. Thousand Oaks, CA: Sage.

Davies, M (2002) *Companion to social work*. Oxford: Blackwell.

Deafblind UK (2009) [online] Available at: **www.deafblinduk.org.uk**

Deafblind UK (2008) **www.deafblind.org.uk**

de Shazer, S (1985) *Keys to solution in brief therapy.* New York: Norton and Company.

Department for Children, Schools and Families (2009) *Safeguarding disabled children: Practice guidance*. London: HM Government.

Department for Children, Schools and Families (2003) *Every Child Matters* **www.dcsf. gov.uk/**

Department of Health and Department for Education and Employment (1999) *The Quality Protects Programme: Transforming Children's Services 2000/01*. Health Service Circular 9HSC(99)237), Local Authority Circular (LAC(99)33) and DfEE Circular No. 18/99. London: Department of Health.

Department of Health (2009a) *Personalised budgets*. London: The Stationery Office.

Department of Health (2009b) *Valuing people now* [online] Available at: **www.dh.gov.uk/ en/Consultations/LiveConsultations/**

Department of Health (2007) *Putting people first: A shared vision and commitment to the transformation of adult social care*. London: The Stationery Office.

Department of Health (2007) *Aiming high for disabled children: Better support for families*. London: The Stationery Office.

Department of Health (2006) *Our health, our care, our say* ([online] Available at: **www. dh.gov.uk/en/Healthcare/**

Department of Health, Home Office, Department for Education and Employment (2006) *Working together to safeguard children: A guide to inter-agency working to safeguard and promote the welfare of children*. London: The Stationery Office.

Department of Health (2005a) *Identification and notification*. London: The Stationery Office.

Department of Health (2005b) *Independence, well-being and choice* [online] Available at: **www.dh.gov/en/Publicationsandstatistics/**

Department of Health (2005c) *Delivering race equality in mental health care: A summary.* London: Department of Health.

Department of Health (2004) *Every Child Matters*: *Change for Children*. London: The Stationery Office.

Department of Health (2003) *Fair access to care services* (FACS). London: The Stationery Office.

Department of Health (2002) *Requirements for social work training.* London: Department of Health.

Department of Health (2001) *Valuing People* [online] Available at: **www.valuingpeople.gov.uk**

Department of Health (2000a) *Framework for the Assessment of Children in Need and their Families*. London: The Stationery Office.

Department of Health (2000b) *No secrets* [online] Available at: **www.dh.gov.uk/en/Publicationsandstatistics/**

Department of Work and Pensions (2005) *Opportunity Age* [online] Available at: **www.dwp.gov.uk/opportunity_age**

Derrida, J (1976) *Of grammatology*. Baltimore, MD: John Hopkins University Press.

Egan, G (2002) *The skilled helper*: *A problem-management and opportunity-development approach to helping.* Seventh edition. Pacific Grove, CA: Brooks/Cole.

Egan, G (1990) *The skilled helper: A systemic approach to effective helping*. Pacific Grove, CA: Brooks/Cole.

Fernando, S (2001) *Mental health, race and culture.* Basingstoke: Palgrave Macmillan.

Fernando, S (1988) *Race and culture in psychiatry*. London: Tavistock/Routledge.

Fiske, J (1994) General editor's preface. In Thompson, N (2003) *Communication and language. A handbook of theory and practice.* Basingstoke: Palgrave Macmillan.

Fiske, J (1990) *Introduction to communication studies*. Second edition. London: Routledge.

Fletcher, L (1987) *Language for Ben. A Deaf child's right to sign.* London: Souvenir Press (Educational and Academic).

Flynn, M and Saleem, J (1986) Adults who are mentally handicapped and living with their parents: Satisfactions and perceptions regarding their lives and circumstances. *Journal of Mental Deficiency Research*, (**30**), 379–87.

Fonagy, P, Steele, M, Steele, H, Higgit, A and Target, M (1994) The theory and practice of resilience. *Journal of child psychology and psychiatry*, 35 (2), 231–57.

Fook, J and Askeland, GA (2007) Challenges of critical reflection: 'Nothing ventured, nothing gained'. *Social Work Education*, 26(5), 520–33.

Fortinash, KM and Worrett, PAH (eds) (2004) *Psychiatric mental health nursing*. Third edition. St Louis, MI: Mosby Publications.

Foucault, M (1999) Space, power and knowledge', in Thompson, N (2003) *Communication and language: A handbook of theory and practice*. Basingstoke: Palgrave Macmillan.

French, S and Swain, J (2007) *Understanding disability: A smile for health professionals*. London: Elsevier Health Sciences.

Gallaudet University www.gallaudet.edu/

General Social Care Council (2001) *Codes of Practice*. Available at: **www.gscc.org.uk**

Glynn, M, Beresford, P, Bewley, C, Branfield, F, Butt, J, Croft, S, Dattani Pitt, K, Fleming, J, Flynn, R, Parmore, C, Postle, K and Turner, M (2008) *Person centred support: What practitioners and service users say*. York: Joseph Rowntree Foundation.

Goldberg, D and Huxley, P (1992) *Common mental disorders: A bio-social model*. London: Routledge.

Golightley, M (2008) *Social work and mental health*. Third edition. Exeter: Learning Matters.

Gracer, BL (2003) What the rabbis heard: Deafness in the mishnah. *Disability Studies Quarterly*, Spring.

Green, G, Hayes, C, Dickinson, D, Whittaker, A and Gilheany, B (2003) A mental health service user's perspective to stigmatisation. *Journal of Mental Health*. June 2003, 12 (3), 223–34.

Guirdham, M (1999) *Communicating across cultures*. London: Macmillan.

Gutman, C (2007) The challenges and rewards of parenthood: Experiences of disabled parents in Israel. *Disability Studies Quarterly*, 27 (4),1–17.

Hales, R and Yudofsky, S (eds) (2004) *Essentials of clinical psychiatry*. Second edition. Washington, DC: American Psychiatric Publishing Inc.

Health and Social Care Information Centre (2008) First report and experimental statistics from Mental Health Minimum Dataset (MHMDS) annual returns 2003 and 2007. *Mental Health Bulletin*.

Healy, K (2005) *Social work theories in context. Creating frameworks for practice*. Basingstoke: Palgrave Macmillan.

Hearing Concern (2007) [online] Available at: **www.hearingconcern.org.uk**

Heenan, D (2005) Challenging stereotypes surrounding disability and promoting anti-oppressive practice: some reflections on teaching social work students in Northern Ireland. *Social Work Education*, 24 (5), 495–510.

Higgins, PC (1980) *Outsiders in a hearing world – A sociology of deafness*. London: Sage.

Hindley, P and Kitson, N (2000) *Mental health and deafness*. London: Whurr Publishers.

History of Education (2004) **www.know-britain.com/**

Holloway, F (1990) Caring for people: a critical review of British government policy for the community care of the mentally ill. *Psychiatric Bulletin,* 14, 641–5.

Horwarth, J (2004) *The child's world: Assessing children in need*. London: Jessica Kingsley.

Howe, D (2001) Attachment. In Horwath, J (ed) (2001) *The child's world: Assessing children in need*. London: Jessica Kingsley.

Howe, D (1987) *An introduction to social work theory*. Aldershot: Gower.

Hudson, J, Hiripi, E, Pope Jr, H and Kessler, R (2006) The prevalence and correlates of eating disorders in the national comorbidity survey replication. *Biological Psychiatry*, 61 (3), 348–58.

Hugman, R (2003) Professional ethics in social work: Living with the legacy. *Australian Social Work,* 56 (1), 5–15.

Jenkins JM and Smith, MA (1990) Factors protecting children in disharmonious homes: Maternal reports. *Journal of the American Academy of Child and Adolescent Psychiatry,* 29,(1), 60–9.

Johns, R (2009) *Using the law in social work.* Fourth edition. Exeter: Learning Matters.

Johns, R (2005) *Using the law in social work.* Second edition. Exeter: Learning Matters.

Jones, C (2001) Voices from the front line: State social workers and new labour. *British Journal of Social Work*, 31(4), 547–62.

Joseph Rowntree Foundation [online] Available at: **www. joseph.rowntree.org.uk**

Jowitt, M and O'Loughlin, S (2007) *Social work with children and families.* Exeter: Learning Matters.

Kadushin, A and Kadushin, G (1997) *The social work interview*. Fourth edition. New York: Columbia University Press.

Keen, S, Gray, I, Parker, J, Galpin, D and Brown, K (2009) *Newly qualified social workers: A handbook for practice.* Exeter: Learning Matters.

Kirby, L and Fraser, M (1997) *Risk and resilience in childhood*, in Horwarth, J (2004) *The child's world*. London: Jessica Kingsley.

Kitson, N and Fry R (1990) Prelingual deafness and psychiatry. *British Journal of Hospital Medicine*, 44, 353–6.

Koprowska, J (2005) *Communication and interpersonal skills in social work*. Exeter: Learning Matters.

Kübler-Ross, E (1970) *On death and dying.* London: Tavistock.

Laming, H (2003) *The Victoria Climbié Inquiry Report. Cm5730.* London: The Stationery Office. Crown copyright. **www.victoria-climbie-inquiry.org.uk**

Le Riche, P and Tanner, K (1998) *Observation and its application to social work: Rather like breathing.* London: Jessica Kingsley.

Levey, G (1997) Hidden from sight? The access of multiple-disabled people to services for the visually impaired. *British Journal of Visual Impairment*, 15 (3). [online] Available at: **www.visugate.biz** In Williams, P (2006) *Social work and people with learning difficulties*. Exeter: Learning Matters.

Lezzoni, L, Ramanan, RA and Drews, RE (2005) Teaching medical students about communicating with patients who have sensory or physical disabilities. *Disability Studies Quarterly*, Issue 1.

Lewis, G and Appleby, L (1988) Personality disorder: the patients psychiatrists dislike. *British Journal of Psychiatry*, 153, 44–9.

Lindesmith, A, Anselm R, Strauss, and Denzin, NK (1975) *Social psychology.* Hinsday, IL: Dryden Press.

Lishman, J (1994) *Communication in social work.* Basingstoke: Macmillan/BASW.

London Safeguarding Children Board (LSCB) (2009) Haringey Executive Summary February 2009 [Online]. Baby P. Available at: **www.dh.gov.uk/enPublicationsandstatistics/**

Lorenz, K (1952) *King Solomon's ring; new light on animal ways.* New York: Crowell.

Macdonald AM (1972) *Chambers New Compact Dictionary*: London: W and R Chambers.

MacNeil, G and Stewart, C (2000) Crisis intervention with school violence problems and volatile situations, in Roberts, AR (2005) *Crisis intervention handbook.* New York: Oxford University Press.

Madsen, WJ (1974) *You have to be Deaf to understand* (Poem). First published in the *British Deaf News*, 9 (8), 253, April.

Maynard, C (2003) Differentiate depression from dementia. *Nurse Practitioner*, March.

McGovern, D and Cope, R (1987) The compulsory detention of males of different ethnic groups, with special reference to offender patients. *British Journal of Psychiatry*, 150, 505–12.

Mind (2006) *Understanding postnatal depression*, London: Mind Publications.

Mitchell, D and Snyder, S (1996) Vital signs: Crip culture talks back. A 48-minute open captioned video produced by Brace Yourself Productions, Marquette, Michigan, in Peters, S (2000) Is there a disability culture? A syncretisation of three possible world views. *Disability and Society*, (4), 583–601.

Morris, J (1995) *Gone missing? A research and policy review of disabled children living away from their families.* London: Who Cares? Trust.

Munro, E (1999) Common errors of reasoning in child protection work. London: LSE Research Articles [online]. Available at: **http://eprints.lse.ac.uk/**

Murphy, C (1999) Loss of olfactory function in dementing disease. *Physiology and Behaviour*, 66, 177–82.

National Autistic Society [online] Available at: **www.nas.org.uk**

National Deaf Children's Society [online] Available at: **www.ndcs.org.uk**

National Institute for Mental Health in England (NIHME) and the Department of Health (DoH) (2005) *Mental health and deafness: Towards equity and access. Best Practice guidelines.* London: Department of Health.

National Occupational Standards [online] Available at: **www.standards.dfes.gov.uk/learningmentors/nos**

NSPCC [online] Available at: **www.nspcc.org.uk/**

Office of National Statistics (2000) *Psychiatric morbidity among adults living in private households in Great Britain*. London: Office of National Statistics.

Office of Public Sector Information [online] Available at: **www.opsi.gov.uk/Acts/**

Oliver, M (1996) *Understanding disability: From theory to practice*. Basingstoke: Macmillan.

Oliver, M and Sapey, B (2006) *Social work with disabled people.* Basingstoke: Palgrave Macmillan.

Osmo, R and Landau, R (2006) The role of ethical theories in decision making by social workers. *Social Work Education*, 25(8), 863–76.

Owusu-Bempah, K and Howitt, D (2000) *Psychology beyond western perspectives.* Leicester: The British Psychological Society.

Parker, J and Bradley, G (2007) *Social work practice: Assessment, planning, intervention and review*. Second edition. Exeter: Learning Matters.

Parrott, L (2007) *Values and ethics in social work practice*. Exeter: Learning Matters.

Payne, M (2005) *Modern social work theory*. Third edition. Basingstoke: Palgrave Macmillan.

Percival, J and Hanson, J (2005) I'm like a tree from the water's edge: Social care and inclusion of older people with visual impairment. *British Journal of Social Work,* (35), 189–205.

Peters, S (2000) Is there a disability culture? A syncretisation of three possible world views. *Disability and Society*, 4, 583–601.

Piaget, J (1936) *Origins of intelligence in the child*. London: Routledge and Kegan Paul.

Postle, K (2002) Working 'between the idea and the reality': Ambiguities and tensions in care managers' work. *British Journal of Social Work*, 32, 335–51.

Priestley, M (2003) *Disability: A life course approach*. Oxford: Blackwell Publishing.

Pritchard, C (2006) *Mental health social work: Evidence-based practice*. Abingdon: Routledge.

Quinney, A (2006) *Collaborative social work practice.* Exeter: Learning Matters.

Reid, WJ (1985) *Family problem-solving*. New York: Columbia University Press.

Reid, W and Epstein, L (1977) *Task-centred practice*. New York: Columbia University Press.

Reid, WJ and Epstein, L (1972) *Task-centred casework*. New York: Columbia University Press.

Reid, W and Shyne, A (1969) *Brief and extended casework*. New York: Columbia University Press.

Richards, S (2000) Bridging the divide: Elders and the assessment process. *British Journal of Social Work*, 30, 37–49.

RNIB Braille www.rnib.org.uk/

RNID [online] Available at: **www.rnid.org.uk/**

RNID [online] Available at: **www.informationline@rnid.org.uk**

Roberts, AR (2000) *Crisis intervention handbook.* Second edition. New York: Oxford University Press.

Robson, C (2007) *How to do a research project. A guide for undergraduate students.* Oxford: Blackwell Publishing.

Rogers, CR (1957) The necessary and sufficient conditions of therapeutic personality change. *Journal of Consulting Psychology*, 21(2), 95–103.

Royal National Institute for Deaf People (2001, 2007) [online] Available at: **www.rnid. org.uk**

Rosenhan, DL (1973) On being sane in insane places. *Science*, 179, 250–8.

Royal National Institute for the Blind RNIB [online] Available at: **www.rnib.org.uk**

Sacks, O (1991) *Seeing voices.* London: Pan Macmillan.

Scheff, T (1999) Preface to *Being mentally ill: A sociological theory.* Third edition. Chicago, IL: Aldine.

Scheff, T (1966) *Being mentally ill: A sociological theory.* Chicago, IL: Aldine.

Schön, DA (1987) *Educating the reflective practitioner.* London: Temple Smith.

Schön, DA (1983) *The reflective practitioner.* New York: Basic Books.

SENSE [online] Available at: **www.sense.org.uk**

SENSE (2007) *Seeing me. Fill in the gaps,* June, 1–25.

Shannon, C and Weaver, W (1947) in Thompson, N (2003) *Communication and language. A handbook of theory and practice.* Basingstoke: Palgrave Macmillan.

Sheldon, B (1995) *Cognitive-behavioural therapy: Research, practice and philosophy.* London: Routledge.

Social Care Institute for Excellence (2004) *Teaching and learning communication skills in social work education.* Bristol: The Policy Press.

Social Justice [online] Available at: **socialjustice.ekduniya.net**

Stanley, N and Manthorpe, J (2004) *The age of inquiry. Learning and blaming in health and social care.* Abingdon: Routledge.

Swain, J, French, S, Barnes, C and Thomas, C (2007) *Disabling barriers – Enabling environments.* Second edition. London: Sage.

Tanner, K and Le Riche, P (1998) *Observation and its application to social work. Rather like breathing.* London: Jessica Kingsley.

Tembe, FM (2009) Research on the violation of human rights of deaf people in Mozambique (famod@kepa.co.mz) **www.disabilityworld.org/**)

Thompson, N (2006) *Anti-discriminatory practice.* Fourth edition. Basingstoke: Palgrave Macmillan.

Thompson, N (2003) *Communication and language: A handbook of theory and practice.* Basingstoke: Palgrave Macmillan.

Thompson, N (1996) *People skills: a guide to effective practice in human services.* Basingstoke: Macmillan Press.

Thomson, GOB, Ward, KM and Wishart, JG (1995) The transition to adulthood for children with Down's Syndrome. *Disability and Society,* 10(3), 325–71.

Trevithick, P (2005) *Social work skills: A practice handbook.* Second edition. Maidenhead: Open University Press/McGraw-Hill Education.

Truax, C and Carkhuff, R (1967) *Towards effective counselling and psychotherapy: Training and practice.* Chicago, IL: Aldine.

Tyrer, P and Steinberg, D (1998) *Models for mental disorder.* Third edition. Chichester: John Wiley & Sons.

Union of the Physically Impaired Against Segregation (1976) *Fundamental principles of disability.* London: UPIAS.

Valios, N (2009*) Opportunity of a lifetime.* Community Care [online] Available at: **www.communitycare.co.uk**

Walker, J, Crawford, K and Parker, J (2008) *Practice education in social work: A handbook for practice teachers, assessors and educators.* Exeter: Learning Matters.

Wallcraft, J and Nettle, M (2009) History, context and language. In Wallcraft, J, Schrank, B and Amering, M (eds) *Handbook of service user involvement in mental health research.* Chichester: John Wiley & Sons.

Walsh, HC (2007) Caring for bereaved people 1: Models of bereavement. *Nursing Times,* 103 (51), 26–7.

Walter, T (1996) A new model of grief: Bereavement and biography. *Mortality,* 1 (1), 7–25.

Warren, J (2007) *Service user and carer participation in social work.* Exeter: Learning Matters.

Watzlawick, P, Weakland, J and Risch, R (1974) *Change: Principles of problem formation and problem resolution.* London: Norton.

Williams, P (2009) *Social work with people with learning difficulties.* Second edition. Exeter: Learning Matters.

Williams, P (2004) Incorporating Social Role Valorisation into other contexts of needs assessment, anti-oppressive practice and the application of values. *International Journal of Disability, Community and Rehabilitation,* 3 (1) **www.ijdcr.ca**

Wilks, T (2005) Social work and narrative ethics. *British Journal of Social Work,* 35: 1249–64.

World Health Organisation (2009) [online] Available at: **www.who.int/en/**

World Health Organisation (1992) *The ICD-10 classification of mental and behavioural disorders.* Geneva: World Health Organisation.

Index

Q10

LEARNING
RESOURCES
CENTRE

HAVERING

This book is due for return on or before the last date shown below.

**For enquiries or renewal at
Quarles Campus LRC
Tel: 01708 462759**